CLERGY SELF-CARE

Finding A Balance for Effective Ministry

ROY M. OSWALD

AN ALBAN INSTITUTE PUBLICATION

Published in association with Ministers Life — A Mutual Life Insurance Company.

Library of Congress Catalog Card # 90-86201
ISBN 1-56699-044-0

07   06   05   04   03   WP   9   10   11   12   13   14   15   16   17   18

CONTENTS

To: My dear friend and mentor

May this bless you as much as it has me – you deserve the best! Praying God's continued favor on you!

Carlito

ACKNOWLEDGMENTS

Just prior to the publication of this book I was involved in a serious automobile accident. Someone previously charged with driving while intoxicated ran a stop sign and hit my car broadside. The crash blew out three of my four tires and so totaled my car that the emergency workers had to cut the doorposts and peel back the roof to get me out. Seeing the car, many wondered how I managed to emerge with only a torn diaphragm, several broken ribs, a fractured sacrum (backbone), and lacerations on my elbow. Surgeons reset all my internal organs (my stomach and intestines were up near my heart) and sewed up my diaphragm. I spent five days in intensive care and six in a regular hospital bed. At this writing, I am home maneuvering on crutches while my sacrum mends. Each day I feel myself gaining strength as the pain subsides, and I am able to sleep for longer stretches.

One doesn't emerge from such a near death experience without being transformed. In some ways I feel like an ancient Shaman who entered the edges of the realm of death to bring back the wisdom to be found there. I will never again take for granted a healthy, well-conditioned body. I have a profound sense of what a gift it is to be alive. I have discovered within me a kind of strength and resilience that I didn't know I had. This incident has profoundly changed my life, and I am not yet clear about the full meaning of that transformation.

I was astounded by the way friends, colleagues, and family members surrounded me throughout the ordeal. Even when I had six or seven tubes sticking in my body, people came and laid hands on my wounds and prayed. Many congregations and communities sent cards telling me they were praying for me. I think I've learned something about how to accept and be grateful for the healing love coming my way. The quiet, helpful presence and the gentle touch of my wife, Carole, stands out for me. She can be so fully present when I need her, yet at other times give me the space and freedom I need to work on my own healing.

It was during my convalescence that I gave this book a final reading and found myself listening in a deeper way to my own rhetoric on health and healing. I wrote out several pages of affirmations to help me on my road back to health. I reaffirmed my convictions about putting only healthy food in my body, and I exercised to the limits of my illness. Every day I visualized myself in a completely healthy state. I also vowed to stay in close touch with my support system. As I read the pages that follow, I felt privileged to have been able to write about ways to wholeness that really do work, especially when the chips are down.

Even though people seem to appreciate my books, I do not consider myself a writer. Everything I write needs to be heavily edited, and this current book had to have 150 pages edited out. That tough task was given to a friend and colleague, Kelsey Menehan. As a fellow INFP (MBTI jargon) she understands completely what it is I want to say, but says it with an economy of words. Thank you, Kelsey, for wading into my verbiage and making me sound like a writer. Each time you've done this I think you have turned a sow's ear into a silk purse.

In closing I want to acknowledge one who taught me a kind of toughness in the face of adversity that I needed to draw upon many times through this ordeal—my mother, Frieda Oswald. Mom was able some-how to pass on to me some of that good old-fashioned stoic endurance when faced with pain and despair. It is to her that I wish to dedicate this book. In the book, I tell about Mom's bout with cancer at age eighty and the resources she drew upon to lick the disease. She turned eighty-seven this March and is still a model of the balanced life for me. She always shows up on time for the exercise classes at her nursing home. She continues to ice curl during the winter and lawn bowl in the summer. I know her prayer life remains the source of her courage as she faces the loneliness and fear of aging. Thanks, Mom. You continue to teach me so much.

Roy M. Oswald
April 1991

INTRODUCTION

Al Tollefson was having a hard time listening to Ellen Schwartz talk about her problems with her husband. He had heard her tale of woe countless times. What he wanted and needed to do was confront Ellen about her rigidity and propensity for being righteous and judgmental. But he didn't have the heart or energy to do it. He would hear her out and then, he hoped, escape to the back porch to smoke his pipe and listen to the crickets.

Though Al has just returned from a three-week vacation with his family, he doesn't feel rested. Since coming back, he has been at the church nearly every night. Besides his regular visits to shut-ins and the sick, Al has put in many extra hours getting the stewardship campaign off the ground. Last night, as he was walking out the door for yet another church committee meeting, he told his wife, Ann, "I'm just not ready to get back into this endless routine."

Al is burned out, but he is too frightened to admit it to himself or anyone else. For the past twelve years he has given so much of himself that he has become depleted, cynical, and self-deprecating. His sermons lack vitality. The people he visits in the hospital find him morose. When church attendance dropped slightly, Al panicked and started pushing himself even harder. But all his drivenness feels like wheels spinning in the sand. Rather than forging ahead in a new direction, Al finds himself rushing around trying to keep people happy. He has offered clear leadership in the past, but now, thinking about a new set of priorities seems to demand more energy than he's got. As they say in the trade, even his reserve tank is on empty.

The malaise in Pastor Susan Miller's life is of quite a different nature.

Over a dozen strong contenders, Susan had been selected senior minister of a 620-member congregation in a midwestern suburb. Being called by Holy Comforter was heady stuff, yet Susan had not been feeling well physically for much of her two-year tenure. Last year back spasms put her out of commission for much of Holy Week. Last winter she caught a cold she couldn't shake. And lately, she has been to the doctor with gastrointestinal pains. Strong coffee to get her going in the morning and alcohol to slow her down at night have not helped her stomach problems.

Susan has not coped well with the transition into her parish, mainly because she has been walloped all at once by a series of life changes. Just prior to moving west, Susan and her husband had decided to separate. Their marriage had been troubled for years, and Susan's call to Holy Comforter had simply brought things to a head. Susan's youngest daughter had decided to stay behind with her father so she could finish college. So Susan had moved alone—away from all of her friends and professional colleagues on the East Coast—to her new life and ministry.

The stress of these life changes has left Susan somewhat dysfunctional at certain key points in her ministry. Her perceptions slightly diminished, she has not read accurately the interactions between herself and her parish. Noticing signs and clues from individuals or within groups could have guided her to an easier entry, but she missed key opportunities to gain credibility. At one meeting, she lashed out at a church matriarch—old behavior that usually emerged when she was overtired or stressed. The rift took weeks of visits to mend.

It is an open question whether Susan will survive her entry into this parish. Her inability to deal with her stress has cost her dearly. People's perceptions of their pastor during the first twelve months of ministry often turn into long-term feelings. Susan is in a deadly circle: the more things don't go well, the harder she pushes herself to fix things. The resulting strain on her psyche has been the major source of her physical ailments.

Al and Susan are composite characters, but they accurately reflect pastors I have known. Perhaps they remind you of clergy you have known as well. I have seen dimensions of them in myself. In all of these cases, lack of self-care is at the core of their difficulties.

The good news is there is a way to turn things around. In Parts Two and Three we will revisit Al and Susan and discover how each found the balance needed for greater personal health and a more effective ministry.

Balance is the key word here. But how does one maintain balance in a job that demands so much of us? After all, we are dealing with what gives life meaning. We are engaged with people and causes that are greater than ourselves. Such deep caring costs us something. At times, we might willingly sacrifice our personal health for the sake of love or growth.

Of course, we all know clergy who are so self-absorbed that the idea of sacrificing for people or causes is the furthest thing from their minds. Their emotional insecurity preempts any kind of spiritual depth. But the clergy who weigh heavily on my heart right now are the best and bright-est, the ones whose zeal for ministry has catapulted them into self-destructive patterns. They have gone like lambs to the slaughter because they have not been offered even minimal survival skills in their training for ministry. And their denominations give little support in self-care. The message they hear from the church at all levels—and from them-selves—is "you can do more" and "you can do it better." Few voices ask, "Are you having any fun lately?" "What is happening to your relationships as a result of your ministry?" "What impact has your ministry had on your body?" "Where are you getting spiritual feeding?"

With no encouragement or support in self-care, clergy are left to twist in the wind. It is only after they are burned out that some clergy scramble out of the boiling cauldron and find saner professions. Those who remain pastors often plug along in cynical exhaustion.

I hope this book will be like a strong rope for some of you to grab onto. I'd like to see whether we can stay in ministry without selling our souls. Perhaps if we come to understand that redemption has already been accomplished, we won't need to sacrifice our bodies to be faithful to ministry.

For others of you, this book will be a challenge. Self-care means taking on some of our toughest, most destructive patterns because if we fail to deal with our addictions or neurotic habits, we diminish our effectiveness as channels of Grace. Of course, ultimately, Grace delivers us from all our foolish ways. Yet on this side of Glory, especially when we are called to be communicators of good news, Grace is what gives us the courage to confront our brokenness. Grace is not an excuse for finding an easy way out. Self-care means facing into the pain and confusion in our lives. It means taking on our pathologies one at a time.

I believe that the nature of parish ministry today requires us to move consistently toward greater health and wholeness. When we get stuck in our personal journey to wholeness, that point of "stuckness" will throw up roadblocks in our ministry. There is simply no way to get around them; we must dismantle them piece by piece.

The Rationale for Self-Care: Some Basic Assumptions

In approaching the topic of stress, burnout, and the need for self-care, I am making several assumptions about pastors' ministries and roles:

I. As Clergy, We Are in the Health and Wholeness Business. The healthier we become on this journey toward wholeness, the more effective we become in our ministry to others. Wholeness happens on four levels simultaneously:

Physical
Emotional
Spiritual
Intellectual

Though our primary focus is on spiritual health—reconciling persons to God and to each other—we intervene in people's lives when they experience ill health in any one of the above areas. Therefore our effectiveness in ministry in each of the four areas is directly proportional to our own wholeness in these areas. Anything we do to increase our health in one of the four areas automatically increases our health in the remaining three.

II. Who and What We Are as Persons Is Our Most Effective Tool in Pastoral Ministry. Marshall McLuhan is right when he states that the "medium is the message." Who we are as persons in ministry speaks much louder than words.

III. Optimal Health Will Be Different for Each Individual. Our spiritual task is to take the cards life dealt us and still be grateful, joyful, and humble. The key to our health and wholeness is coping well with the stresses of life and warding off the debilitating effects of burnout. (Stress and burnout are different phenomena, which we will discriminate.) Few of us are able to face the pain of our ill health without massive support from individuals and communities. The path that leads to health and wholeness always seems too formidable or too demanding. We will all try unproductive paths before we face squarely our addictions and neuroses.[1]

IV. Our Work with Congregations Needs to Be Systemic and Wholistic, Applying the Above Principles to Parish Life. To support and encourage health in congregational life, we must place healthy clergy in their midst. Our task as congregations is to grow into healthy systems in which broken and dysfunctional people can find healing. Our effec-tiveness as congregations in dealing with the pain and brokenness in society is directly proportional to the congregation's health as a whole and the individual health of its clergy and laity.

V. As Clergy, We Need to Reclaim Our Role in the Healing Arts. Modern medicine has trivialized our role in helping people pursue physical health. Spiritual healing is often the prerequisite to healing on an emotional or physical level. Congregations are in a strong position to be involved in wholistic health efforts, which counter what I believe is a dysfunctional "medical model" that treats pathology in isolation from the whole person.[2]

These basic assumptions are autobiographical, reflecting my own struggle with my addictions, neuroses, and brokenness as I have tried to be a model and mentor to clergy and key lay leaders. The feed-back from participants at events I lead affirms that I am most effective when I take the risk of revealing some of the battle that continually rages inside me. I am also aware that the healthier I become, the greater the respect and attention afforded me. I am confident that the same will be true of you as you apply some of the principles of self-care in this book. Here's your invitation to a healthier you and a more dynamic ministry.

PART ONE

Self-Care and the Ministry

CHAPTER 1

What They See Is What They Get

Each of us makes a powerful theological statement the moment we enter a room. People take one look at us and immediately determine something about our self-image, how we are managing our sexuality, the level of our self-care, our openness to learn and grow, our enthusiam or lack of it, etc.. How do they make such a judgment? Theorists claim that only fifteen percent of what we communicate is verbal; the rest—eighty-five percent—comes through nonverbally.

The fact that so much is communicated nonverbally should be sobering—and challenging—to us as clergy. Exactly what are we communicating through our body language, facial expressions, posture, skin tone, eyes, voice tone and texture, speed or slowness of speech, gestures, dress, intensity and affect, breathing rate, level of fatigue or vitality? Whether we like it or not, our health (or lack of it) is out there for all the world to see.

It is very difficult for us to be agents of good news when we are either stressed out or burned out. We may say all the right things from the pulpit, but communicate the opposite. A stressed-out pastor like Susan Miller may think she is responding to people in a loving way, but her nonverbals will give away the stress in her body every time. When a burned-out pastor, like Al Tollefson, makes a hospital call, he may say the right words and pray the right kind of prayer, but still communicate that he would rather be somewhere else. It's a double message, and the nonverbal message usually predominates.

Approximately twenty percent of clergy with whom I've worked in seminars score extremely high on the Clergy Burnout Inventory (See Chapter 8). Among clergy in long pastorates (ten years or more) the number jumps to fifty percent. The number is lower for younger clergy who generally score higher on stress scales than on the burn-out inventory. The tragedy is that our best clergy—the hard-working, dedicated folk who have given too much of themselves for too long without replenishing the cup—are burning out. These burned-out clergy usually become dull, hollow, and uninteresting. When you meet them there is little to excite you. You don't want to get to know them better.

A pastor in this condition will not attract people in droves to his or her church. The Alban Institute Study on Assimilation of New Members discovered that newcomers wanted to "get a fix" on the clergy-person very early on. They wanted to know whether or not the pastor was a "good enough" religious authority: Was she trustworthy? Did he have a quality of being? Did she express a sense of caring that felt authentic? Newcomers "sized up" the pastor more by what he communicated non-verbally than by what was said. Even if newcomers were attracted to a parish for other reasons, they would not join unless they felt good about the pastor.[1]

What are you communicating to your congregation right now? Overwhelming tiredness or a sense of being grateful to be alive and to be in ministry with God's people? If your energy level is low, getting the words just right won't make a difference. If you're upset or distraught, working harder and smiling stiffly won't fool anybody. No wonder many clergy have a recurring dream (or nightmare) of leading Sunday morning worship while stark naked. The old hymnbook just isn't big enough to hide behind.

The only way we will be a healthy presence among our people is to keep ourselves healthy. That's where self-care comes in—doing all that is necessary to win out against the twin destroyers, stress and burnout.

Narcissism vs. Self-Care

In seminars with pastors, I often feel the tension in the room rise when the subject of self-care comes up. It just doesn't set right with some clergy. Some unconscious tapes play in their minds telling them that taking care of self is somehow unChristian or at least unnecessary. That certainly was true for me. Early on the message was hammered home that the acceptable route in life involved sacrifice and hard work. In my family you could get your ears pulled if you got too hung up on yourself.

Combine this early upbringing with a theology of commitment and sacrifice for the sake of the Gospel, and self-care got pushed down very low on the totem pole.

Given these unconscious processes, it's no wonder that clergy who *do* take care of themselves are sometimes viewed suspiciously. They're taking the soft path, rather than the path we've been taught is the right one—the one with all the thorns and rocks. Yet self-care, rightly understood, does not imply copping out and retiring to a lawn chair for the rest of our lives. We must hold on to the notion that the ordained ministry is special and costly. Ministry is not going to work if it refuses to engage with people who are struggling. Preaching at people from an antiseptic place of safety just won't cut it. At the same time, failing to be a good steward of our life and health won't do ourselves or our ministries any good either.

Another reason clergy seem to resist greater self-care is their fears about being identified with the "me" generation. Clergy born before the baby boom period seem to be particularly sensitive about this. It is true that a kind of narcissism plagues prosperous western cultures. Some would call it an epidemic. Many people *are* totally self-indulgent. *After all*, they say, *isn't life, liberty, and the pursuit of happiness our right?* They become so absorbed with themselves that they fail to see life as a gift, relationships as Grace, and meaningful work as a privilege. They miss the point that the foundation of prayer is gratitude and instead demand of God what they regard as rightfully theirs.

Self-care can become destructive self-indulgence, but it can also be quite different from that. Again, we need to strike some kind of balance. We'll never get the balance exactly right, and when we do, it won't last long because some new stressor will tip the scale again. But working at that balance day by day pays off in the long run.

For me, self-care is little more than being a steward of some rather special gifts—a physical body with its enormous resilience and beauty, the capacity to nurture others and be nurtured in return, the capacity to be aware of our lives as we are living them, the capacity to enjoy immense sensual pleasure through such simple things as the splash of orange juice in our throats in the morning or a child on our lap.

I like to think of self-care as a commitment we make to God when we accept the role of resident religious authority. When we accept the call to be an agent of Grace, we simultaneously promise to forgo the easy life of self-indulgence, which can be a stumbling block to God's agents. I have come to call this "self-care for the sake of the kingdom." I take care of myself, not only for my sake, or in gratitude for the life given me by God, but also for the sake of others. If I don't take care of myself, I not only hurt myself, but I let others down as well.

At clergy workshops, I sometimes ask participants, "Would you feel some anger if you paid a handsome tuition to attend an Alban Institute seminar led by Roy Oswald, and I showed up sixty pounds overweight, my clothes reeking from smoke, and seemingly depressed and distracted?" Usually participants say "yes," they would feel cheated. Members of our congregations probably are similarly disappointed when they come to church and their pastor is too stressed to listen to them and too burned out to show any real caring.

What does good self-care look like? The term optimum health may provide some glimpses. This means striving for the best that we can be given our age, genes, liabilities and disabilities, and life experiences. Forget about trying to be like Tom Selleck or Princess Diana. What are the attitudes, disciplines, and lifestyles that bring out the best in us?

You may think, "I'm fifty-five, short, bald, walk with a limp, and have a hooked nose." Well, let's look at two clergy who fit that description. One remains trim and has, through therapy and a quality support group, gained a positive self-image. He has found ways to consistently deepen his spiritual side. Parishioners love his vitality and sense of humor. The older women in the congregation think of him as sexy and attractive.

The other pastor with similar statistics is overweight, depressed, cynical, and just trying to hang on until retirement. There is a myth in most denominations that pastors over age fifty don't receive calls to another church. I believe that the first pastor I described, once he gets an initial interview, would receive a call. The second pastor probably wouldn't. The difference between the two is obvious and it has to do with how they take care of themselves.

For me, optimum health means managing our lives in such a way that we consistently maintain our physical, emotional, intellectual, and spiritual well-being. Helen Keller was the best she could be even though she was both blind and deaf. Someone in a wheelchair, paralyzed from the neck down, can be a constant delight because of her humor and spiritual depth. Whatever cards life has dealt us—our genes, our family of origin, our traumas and tragedies, our friends—the spiritual task before us is to take that stack of cards and shuffle them in such a way that we come up positive, joyful, grateful, and humble. Then, we can offer ourselves to church and society.

I believe our chief task here on earth is to learn and grow. Unfortunately, in our culture we usually think of learning and growing strictly in terms of our intellects. So we have bright, capable people who are infantile in their emotional lives, shallow spiritually, and unable to manage the cravings and addictions of their bodies. As they consistently sabotage themselves with their excesses, we shake our heads: "She has so much to offer."

We need to learn to take care of ourselves in all areas of our lives, finding that balance between healthy self-care and unhealthy narcissism. Sometimes that process may get downright complicated. For example, there may be times when we are working through a difficult passage in our lives and our bodies simply need more sleep. Stress can be quite demanding on the body and psyche, and fatigue is to be expected. At such times it's important to give ourselves permission to sleep in. There are other times, however, when what our body really needs is a brisk walk before breakfast, not a few more minutes in a warm bed. We need to be able to discern what our bodies are really telling us.

If all of this sounds too difficult, it need not be. There will be aspects of wellness that are harder for us. Yet after the struggle, there comes the joy of feeling good. In fact, we may reach levels of joy we never thought possible. From this place of wellness, we can feel confident in inviting others to join us. It is out of this crucible that effective ministry comes.

CHAPTER 2

What It Means to Be in the Health and Wholeness Business

Amidst the many and sometimes seemingly impossible demands of pastoral ministry, we have opportunities to intervene in people's lives in ways unknown to other professionals. Sure, we have to earn our credibility with parishioners. It is not something conferred upon us just because we are pastors. Even so, we have unusual access to people. We can walk into people's offices or visit them in their homes and voice our concerns about what is happening in their lives. They may not agree with us, but more than likely they will give us a hearing and perhaps even thank us for our concern. There is no other role in society that has that kind of access or authority.

Of course, parishioners expect clergy to guide them in their spiritual lives, but that is not the limit of our influence. We interact with people when they have physical, emotional, and intellectual concerns as well. When people are sick, we visit them in the hospital or at home and are expected to pray for them. When people have emotional problems, we make ourselves available for pastoral counseling. When people don't understand their life situation, we help them think things through intellectually so they can function better. (In fact, pastors soon learn that the doorway to a person's spiritual life is often through one of the other dimensions.) Clergy are still at the top of the list of those individuals turn to when they have a problem.

The ministry is one of the only true generalist professions left in our society. While all other professions are becoming more and more specialized, we as clergy are still given authority to look at the whole picture—one's body stewardship, the quality of one's relationships, one's values, beliefs, and morals. Being a generalist may feel uncomfortable at times because we are not able to claim expertise in one slice

of life. As a parish pastor, I longed to do something specific and concrete for people, like stitching up a wound or facilitating a loan. At times
I forgot that my specialty was being the lover who cared about the total
well-being of my parishioners.

What it comes down to is this: as generalists, we are in the health
and wholeness business. To do well in our generalist role requires that
we work diligently to nurture our own well-being in each of the four
dimensions. If I seriously want to be a better pastor, I first need to ask
myself, "How can I be a healthier, more whole person?" Staying healthy
in each of the four areas is hard, unending work. It's like trying to herd a
flock of sheep through a meadow. You run to one end to get some sheep
in line, then back to the middle, then over to the other side. This year, I
may need to go on a serious diet and embark on an exercise regimen to
get my body in shape. Next year, I may need therapy because my
emotional well-being is in jeopardy. Later on, I may need to get my
brain out of low gear and learn something new. Or the deficit in my life
may be in my spiritual side, with cynicism eating up my days. What I
need is some spiritual counsel to get me out of that hole. Often I'll have
an easier time maintaining health in one or two dimensions than in the
remaining ones. One of the four areas will probably hold me back from
achieving greater total health.

I find it helpful to visualize the components of health on a continuum from one to ten:

Physical Health

- 1_____ 5 _____10 +

Emotional Health

- 1_____ 5 _____10 +

Intellectual Health

-. 1_____ 5 _____10 +

Spiritual Health

- 1_____ 5 _____10 +

When I am in the "below five zone," I am functioning pathologically in that dimension. I may need a professional to help me get to five at least (being functional again). Then I will be able to do things for myself to move higher. Anything you or I do to increase our health in one area automatically increases our health in the remaining three areas. Conversely, when my health diminishes in one area, it negatively affects my health in the remaining areas. On this scale of 1 to 10, with 1 far to the left on the minus side, 5 at the center, and 10 at the end of the plus side, we might rate ourselves as follows: Physical Health—6, Emotional Health —3, Spiritual Health—4, and Intellectual Health—8. This helps focus our attention on what we have going for us in terms of total health and which areas in our lives need work and attention.

Viewing Health Wholistically—A Counterculture Idea

In our culture, ninety-five percent of medical professionals deal mainly with physical pathology. Some would say that doctors know a lot about illness, but very little about health. The economics of our entire health care system are based on this medical model. When we have a pain somewhere, our doctor tells us, "Well, let's do some tests to see what's not working well." With great efficiency, considering the complexity of certain medical problems, they are able to locate the difficulty. Then we take pills or have surgery. Most of the time we become functional again, but physicians usually don't help us reflect on what might be out of kilter in our lives that caused the illness in the first place.

Wholistic health professionals do medical tests, too, but they also help us locate the dysfunctional parts of our lives that might have contributed to our illness. The health care team would ask what we were eating, whether we were exercising, what's happening at our job, whether we were having any fun, how things were going in our family. Because this kind of care takes about five times longer than a traditional doctor's visit, wholistic physicians would make less money—and we would probably not want to pay them for the extra time either. Instead, we make separate appointments with our spiritual director, therapist, physician or surgeon, all of whom operate independently of one another. None of them ever gets the whole picture of our wellness or our illness.

As a result, we learn very little about prevention. To move ourselves from the minus to the plus side of the continuum, we need to look elsewhere. Books, magazine articles, and friends have probably taught you more about such things as diet, exercise, the healing power of laughter, and nutrition than anything you learned from medical professionals.

Where the medical model consistently lets us down is in helping us adopt a healthier life style *before* we get sick. My father never got any medical attention until after he had a major heart attack at age fifty-six. The truth is, his arteries had been corroding for ten years. He was overweight, smoked, ate the same kind of food he grew up on as a farm boy—meat, eggs, butter, fatty desserts—and he exercised sporadically. Yet the first time anyone talked to him about his lifestyle was after he had the heart attack. The medical profession is doing more in the area of prevention these days, but not enough. We need to take responsibility for our overall health and not leave it to others.

Staying healthy emotionally is an equally tough challenge for a parish pastor. It is difficult to keep any kind of emotional equilibrium as we move with our congregations through births, deaths, marriages, divorces, difficulties with children, retirement, etc. In addition, it is difficult to maintain a quality family life when we routinely work sixty to eighty hours each week. And time pressure often precludes clergy being part of a support group that could nurture a healthier emotional life.

Staying healthy intellectually is a challenge for some clergy, too. Many have let their minds go to sleep and haven't cracked a stimulating book in years. According to Mark Rouch in his book *Competent Ministry*,[1] only twenty percent of clergy in the U.S. engage in regular continuing education events of five days or more each year. Matthew Fox claims that the clergy's worst sin against the church is not being heretical or unethical, but being just plain dull.[2] Have we lost the ability to fire the imaginations of the brightest and the best in this country?

Even though religion is our business, staying healthy spiritually remains a significant challenge for clergy. We're supposed to be experts on spiritual matters, but we get little support for taking regular time to feed our spiritual hunger. Throughout seminary, we are fed a steady diet of daily chapel attendance, but are given next to no advice on how to feed ourselves spiritually when we leave the seminary community.

As you might have guessed, I'm unimpressed with the quality of help we get to stay healthy in the physical, emotional, or spiritual realms.

Yet it remains true that the quality of our ministry depends on our consistently pursuing greater health in each of these arenas of life.

Toward a Theology of Self-Care

I had just completed a presentation at one of my pastor seminars on the need for physical exercise to keep the cardiovascular system healthy. Pastor Joe came up to me and said, "There is nothing more boring than exercise."

He was a big man, easily fifty pounds overweight. "Is there anything you like doing?" I asked.

"I like golf," he responded.

"How often do you get to play?" I replied.

"Once a week in warm weather, if I'm lucky. Usually there is something that happens in the parish that pre-empts my game."

As we talked, I discovered that Joe smoked a pack of cigarettes a day and spent sixty to seventy hours a week in the church. Further probing revealed a pretty shaky marriage. I wondered if a little scare tactic might reach him. "Are you aware that you are killing yourself with your lifestyle?" I asked. He responded, "If God wants to take me, I'm ready. Who needs this vale of tears anyway?" His anger and depression were apparent.

Joe is not unlike many of the clergy I meet. Not only are they not taking care of themselves, but they often use a sort of eschatological fatalism to justify their lack of self-care. They feel that if they expend themselves completely in the Lord's work, God will look after them—body, mind, and spirit. Their future is secure. Because the final goal is to be with the Lord, it is all right to mortgage one's body against this final eventuality.

As I've looked at my own life and talked to pastors, it's clear to me that much of what we do in ministry is governed by our theology of ministry. I began my ministry with the idea that I could singlehandedly make the small mission congregation to which I had been called grow and flourish. Seminary had prepared me intellectually for theological and biblical work with parishioners, but it did not prepare me to deal with my limitations in coping with their seemingly insatiable demands and the confusion I felt in trying to set priorities among the many parish tasks. I felt surrounded by a sea of human need that I set out to fill through my own physical resources. My growing despair and anger occasionally surfaced in my sermons. I thought I was being prophetic, but actually I was berating them for not working as hard as I did. I was defenseless against the demands of ministry because I had no theological perspective for self-care and the management of my limitations. I had not yet discovered what it meant to be a wounded healer.

During this time, there were many nights when I wished I could die. Death seemed the only way out of my despair. One night sitting alone in the dark, I felt so lonely and empty that the tears began to flow. My private communion set was on the coffee table. I wondered if I could find solace in giving myself communion, but rejected the idea with the thought that communion was only valid when celebrated within a community. The Grace I preached to others I was unable to apply to myself.

Many pastors caught in this kind of despair simply move on to another parish. If I had done that, I'm convinced I would have repeated the same patterns in a new place. What I needed was a whole new theology of ministry, one which included a theology of self-care. Let's take a look at what such a theology of ministry might look like.

The Call to Ministry

A sound theology of self-care begins with a re-evaluation of the call to ministry. It was rather painful for me as I got in touch with the underlying reasons I entered the ordained ministry in the first place. I became a pastor mostly to please my father and mother and, secondly, to assuage an angry God. Like St. Augustine I considered myself a dreadful sinner because I had powerful sexual feelings, even though I didn't do much about them.

Also, I had this strong need to be needed. I needed the parish ministry to feel like a whole person. With this unconscious motive underlying my call, I was set up to be exploited by any congregation. Rather than doing ministry as a response to an experience of the Grace of God, I was doing it to assuage guilt or to seek some sort of personal fulfillment. When people needed me, my ministry was confirmed.

If our mission is to serve people, we view everyone in need as the voice of God calling us into service. Not to respond is to be guilty of rejecting God's demands upon us. This view of the call of God led me into an adversary relationship with my parishioners. Every time they needed something of me, it was God calling me. But their needs were insatiable. In my exhaustion, I saw my people as the enemy. They were wreaking havoc with my body, my prayer life, my significant relationships. Yet to say "no" to their demands resulted in feelings of guilt for having failed God.

But what if I had viewed God's call first and foremost as an invitation to liberation and wholeness? If I had applied God's Grace to myself first, I might have been able to respond by living a joyful, serene life in the midst of my people. My mission would have been not only to preach the liberating word of Grace to my people, but to model a way for them to live by that Grace. Grace is God's response to our human condition. Part of what it means to be human is to fail, to experience fatigue, to be finite, to need relationships and support. When, out of my own human resources, I attempt to meet this sea of human need around me, I am saying that I'm both omnipotent and omnipresent. These are characteristics of God, not humans. When I live this way, I sin just as Adam and Eve did when they desired to be like God.

I must reinterpret my call to a parish as primarily a call to serve God, not necessarily to serve people. My first call is to be a liberated, whole human being. My first responsibility to my congregation is to be a joyful, redeemed human being. This works only if ministry is viewed as a communal activity with people in mission. We are who we are related to. We cannot maintain our health and wholeness unless there is support for this among our people.

Parishioners need to have a stake in us and our health and well-being. What we offer in return is assistance and support for them to live healthy, whole, and forgiven lives. This gets us out of an adversarial relationship with our people and enables us to join them in living in the light of God's Grace. Then the minister is not the savior, but the one who offers guidance and leadership through his/her own health and wholeness, and in turn is invited to greater wholeness through the health and wholeness of persons in the congregation.

Creation vs. Salvation

A sound theology of ministry also requires us to reassess the meaning of being created by God and saved by God. God created humankind and looked at us and said, "This is very good." Breathing life into the human body was the pinnacle of divine creation. Such a gift the human body is! Combine it with mind and spirit and you have the genius of a whole person. Having bestowed on us the gifts of sensation, intuition, thinking, and feeling, God felt confident enough to make us stewards of the rest of creation. We are called to be overseers of an immense number of inter-connections that make up who we are as persons. Our stewardship extends to management of all the interconnectedness that makes up our environment on this fragile planet. God invites us to honor the sacred rhythm of work and rest, giving us a commandment to move deeply into rest after six days of labor.

Sometimes our doctrine of salvation seems to come into conflict with the doctrine of creation, as if God gives with one hand and takes back with the other. But at its core, the doctrine of salvation is telling us that the world has already been saved. Redemption is complete. For us clergy, this means we don't have to save the world again, much less the people entrusted to our care. When I burn myself out in this ministry, it's usually because I subconsciously believe that salvation is up to me, that, somehow, salvation needs to be redone by me. What freedom comes when we realize that the task of salvation has been accomplished!

A Theology of the Body

As we noted in Chapter 1, our bodies reflect so much more accurately what we believe than our words. We are a walking theological statement before we open our mouths. But most of us don't take our bodies very seriously. We are influenced still by ancient Greek philosophy that saw the body as carnal and weak and the mind and spirit as highly exalted. To the Greeks, the body was something to contend with, as one might contend with leprosy.

The Hebrews, on the other hand, viewed the body as part of the whole. One's body, heart, soul, and mind were all of a piece. The body was not something to be used and eventually disposed of like a Kleenex while the mind and soul remained immortal. As Christians we do not believe in the immortality of the soul only. We also believe in the resurrection of the body. Perhaps we will be able to recover a theology of the body when we become as passionate about it as we are about church doctrine and liturgy. I will believe we have done this when semi-naries open up as much room for dance and exercise as for the library. When we are as concerned with what we feed the body as what we feed our minds, our places of worship will change radically. We will encourage physical expressions of praise, rather than stacking bodies row on row so we can address only people's minds and hearts.

The Kenosis of Christ

Jesus Christ is an excellent example of how to do ministry while taking care of oneself. Jesus didn't allow his caring to completely overextend him so that he had no energy for primary things. He offered himself as a sacrifice for the sake of a broken world, yet in spite of the magnitude of his mission, he did not allow himself to get so strung out that he lost his center and his relationship with God. It was not the intent of the Gospel writers to show us how well Jesus took care of himself. Yet just look at some of the self-care passages that emerge in the Gospel narratives:

Mark 3:7—"Jesus withdrew with his disciples to the sea..."

Luke 9:10—"On their return the apostles told him what they had done. And he took them and withdrew apart to a city called Bethsaida."

Luke 6:12—"In these days he went out to the mountain to pray; and all night he continued in prayer to God."

Luke 5:15—"But so much the more the report went abroad concerning him; and great multitudes gathered to hear and to be healed of their infirmities. *But he withdrew to the wilderness* and prayed."

Matthew 14:22—"Then he made the disciples get into the boat and go before him to the other side, while he dismissed the crowds. And after he had dismissed the crowds, he went up on the mountain by himself to pray. When evening came he was there alone..."

The kenosis of Christ is his decision to empty himself for the sake of the world. He saw clearly the path he needed to take as the suffering servant spoken of in second Isaiah. This feature of Christ's ministry is best summed up in Philippians 2:6-9 where the apostle Paul writes:

...though he was in the form of God, did not count equality with God a thing to be grasped, but emptied himself, taking the form of a servant, being born in the likeness of [humans]. And being found in human form he humbled himself and became obedient unto death, even death on a cross.

From time to time we need to be reminded that the redemption of the world has already been accomplished for us. Our own personal crucifixion will not add one iota to what Christ has already done for us.

Don't get me wrong. I still believe in a theology of the cross. The experience of the cross for clergy has to do with our call to be prophets, servants, and leaders in Christ's Church. There are times when we need to go to the mat on an issue, and if it means some people get upset with us or even leave the church, so be it. We must learn to choose our fights and stay healthy for the battles that really count.

Think about what would have become of Christ's mission if he had allowed himself to be continually exhausted by the poor and the sick, and instead of dealing curtly with the Scribes and Pharisees, had allowed their questions and criticism to demoralize him. What if Jesus had allowed himself to be continually discouraged by the inability of his disciples to get the point of his mission? What if he had become physically and emotionally exhausted, cynical, disillusioned, and self-deprecating? Would that have affected the course of history or influenced your desire to commit your life to him?

Jesus chose kenosis rather than burnout, and because he did we are free to focus energy on primary issues in our parishes. We do not need to be reduced to mush through burnout. Thomas Merton once said that we as clergy need to learn how to say "no" to our people at times or else we will find ourselves supporting their illusions about themselves and the world. As a parish pastor I often found myself overresponding to every need, even the neurotic ones. Since then I've learned that to be a person of compassion, I must not allow myself to become strung out with every human need that comes my way. I invite all of us to continue the struggle to become clearer about the difference between worthwhile priorities and those that merely deplete our energy and do not honor God.

Becoming a Wounded Healer

It may sound like a contradiction, but total health involves embracing our brokenness. Wholeness should never be seen as perfection, but rather an acknowledgment and acceptance of weakness. It has taken me years to understand this.

I left the parish ministry disillusioned and burned out after only four years. But nothing really changed in the way I went about my life and work. I took a position in youth ministry with my denomination, but tackled that job with the same over-functioning style. This time, in addition to planning and executing youth ministry events in Central Pennsylvania and in the national church, there was a war in Vietnam that had to be stopped. If I was to support young people in their stance as conscientious objectors, I had to do my best to end the carnage. I can still feel myself teetering on the edge of burnout as I tried to organize a bunch of liberals to take concrete action against the war. Once again it was all Law and little Grace. Small wonder that I rubbed a lot of people the wrong way in that middle judicatory of 600 churches.

After eight years in the civil rights movement, in addition to my work with the denomination, I hit a midlife crisis that ended my marriage and threw me into four years of heavy psychoanalysis. Even though I wasn't exactly fired, I was strongly encouraged to find a ministry elsewhere. I was offered a job as director of training for the Metropolitan Ecumenical Training Center in Washington, D.C. I left Pennsylvania pretty much a broken person, filled with enormous reservations about the church.

If anything helped me to understand Grace it was landing in an extremely healing environment at the Center. The director of the Center was Tilden Edwards, who had gone through his own midlife crisis and moved from the arena of social action to spiritual direction. I still find Tilden a very positive role model of how a man can let go and experience Grace. During this time I also met Loren Mead, who showed me the relationship between the church and the behavioral sciences. When the training center was dismantled, I began working with The Alban Institute.

In my ministry today, I still feel twinges of that neurotic person from time to time. To help me stay on track I rely heavily on my spiritual director (female) and a long-term support group with three other men, plus an occasional visit with a therapist. These people help me stay in touch with my brokenness and cheer me on when I feel I have something to celebrate. And I bear testimony that my effectiveness as a church professional continues to increase the healthier I become.

Henri Nouwen would describe me as a "wounded healer."[3] I firmly believe that my effectiveness with clergy and key lay leaders comes from having confronted my own pain and confusion earlier in my ministry. I continue to feel the wound of some bad mistakes I've made, yet this woundedness gives me energy to assist others in staying out of the same potholes. I hope I'm providing what one burned-out parish pastor described as "a foothold in the swamp."[4]

There are no shortcuts to wholeness, and the process toward health never ends in this life. That's why it's good to know that our woundedness can be a way of reaching others. In fact, it may be the most important way of all.

PART TWO

The Stress of Ministry

CHAPTER 3

Fill My Cup, Lord, But Not Too Much

In December of 1989 I returned from a ten-day road trip in which I had conducted seminars with four separate groups. I would no sooner terminate with one group than the next one started. Midway through the trip I began to have heart palpitations. If anything raises my stress level even higher than it already is, it's having my heart act funny. I was with my father when he had his first heart attack at age fifty-six, and it's an experience I will never forget. A stroke and a second heart attack took him at age fifty-nine, so I'm aware that the weak link in my genetic code is probably my cardiovascular system.

I had experienced similar palpitations five years previously and ended up in a Washington, D.C. hospital. If anything can give you a heart attack it's finding yourself in the intensive care coronary unit with an intravenous needle sticking in your arm, nitroglycerine taped to your body (which makes your head feel like a three-day hangover) and specialists hovering over you and checking your heart monitor every five minutes. After several days my palpitations stopped, and when the doctors checked me out on the treadmill, they said they hadn't seen such a healthy heart in months. They showed my heart on a television screen: it reminded me of the gentle run of an antelope.

So . . . the palpitations back then had clearly been stress-related. Why were they happening to me again this December? Physician, heal thyself!

I truly appreciate the way my colleagues at The Alban Institute respond when something like this happens to me. Loren Mead makes me get out my datebook and strongly admonishes me to give up a contract or two to ease my workload. The difficulty is that I dearly love my work,

so my Alban colleagues have to sit on me and pry my fingers loose from
"just one more" seminar.

This time the palpitations stopped just before Christmas, and I
haven't had them since. Fortunately, I had planned to take the six weeks
of Lent to write this book. A few cancelled contracts got me past Easter
to when I would again be standing in front of a group talking about
stress. Time to listen to my own rhetoric, which I know works when I
give it a chance.

For years I have been telling people what I have learned about the
effects of stress: that too much stress over too long a period is a major
factor in illness. That at least seventy percent of the ailments doctors
treat may be stress-related.[1] That stress has been related to such physiological illnesses as heart disease, cancer, and hypertension and to such
psychological affects as irritability, depression, and sleep disorders. That
stress can also lead to increased smoking or drinking, overeating, accident proneness, and spouse or child abuse, not to mention other regres-
sions to infantile behavior that can sabotage our lives and our ministries.

Yet, as dire as all that sounds, I also discovered that stress is not
necessarily a bad thing. In fact, much of the time it is a positive force
that keeps us challenged and growing. The trick, for me and for you, is
to maintain life and work styles that avoid either being overstimulated
beyond our threshold level or understimulated so that we rust out (see
Stress Threshold Diagram, page 40). As my experience with the heart
palpitations confirms, that is easier said than done.

Red Alert! How Stress Effects the Body

All types of stress, no matter what their sources, trigger the same physiological responses. When we perceive something unsettling in our environment, the hypothalmus of our brain triggers the autonomic nervous
system and the endocrine-gland system (especially the pituitary, thyroid,
and adrenal glands), which then prepare our bodies to either fight or run.
This fight/flight response is what helped our ancient ancestors deal with
whatever was frightening them in their environment. When our nervous
system hits the alarm, our bodies can sometimes do superhuman things.
I read about several men who were able to lift a car when their buddy
was trapped underneath. The following day, when they tried to repeat
the feat, they couldn't do it.

Most of the time when our bodies signal a response to stress, we aren't being asked to lift a car or do some other heroic deed. Moreover, in these modern times, running away or fighting is often quite inappropriate. Unfortunately, our minds and bodies do not understand this and prepare us anyway. So you're in a meeting and someone begins confronting you about something. You want to chop the person in the mouth or run out of the room, but you can do neither. So you try to listen—actively, of course—while this torrent rages inside. Your blood pressure rises significantly. Your heart begins to beat ra-pidly. Your liver dumps sugar and cholesterol into your bloodstream for extra energy. Your pupils dilate and your stomach stops digesting. Blood from your hands and feet are drawn to the large muscles of your body so that they can function at maximum strength during the perceived emergency. Yet during the rest of the meeting there is no outlet for this stress response. If you're lucky, you may be able to use the energy the next morning to clobber an opponent on a racquetball court.

"The committee listed all the qualities needed in an effective youth pastor.... I wouldn't let a person like this into my house."

An occasional stress reaction, such as the one mentioned above, would hardly place your health in jeopardy—unless, of course, you are on the verge of a heart attack and the confrontation is the final trigger. What becomes exceedingly unhealthy is enduring continual stress throughout our days and weeks. From my experience doing stress seminars with clergy and laity, I'm convinced that the majority of us don't know the level of stress we live with day to day. In the fast-paced industrial West, stressful living is taken for granted. Simply trying to switch lanes on the freeway or watching the evening news can trigger an adrenal response. Add to that all the stress of living with other human beings in close quarters—like our spouses and children and other significant others—and you have a formula for excessive stress.

So if you want less stress, you find a nice calm profession like the ministry, right? Hardly. Pastors are in a people-related profession in which our value to others is our ability to get down in the trenches with them when the bombs are dropping all around. In addition to being there for people through all the joys and traumas of their lives, we are expected somehow, by magic, to keep everybody happy and make our congregations grow. All of this in a post-Christian/Jewish culture that no longer holds in high esteem men and women of the cloth. If we are not stressed, to a greater or lesser degree, we aren't in touch with reality.

Perhaps the best we can hope for is to become models of stress management in our parishes. To do that, first we need to become aware of the specific ways stress affects us (we are all different on this score). Second, we need to pinpoint the specific stressors in our day-to-day ministry. Third, we need to find the self-care strategies that will work to reduce our stress.

I feel fortunate to be able to teach others about stress because it forces me to know myself and "walk my talk." Studying stress has dramatically changed my life. My physical appearance has changed. My weight and muscle tone have changed and so have my recreational habits. I've also radically changed my eating habits over the last eight years and increased the time I spend with friends and family.

Granted, I had a long way to go. In my early years as a parish pastor, migraine headaches, an upset stomach, fatigue, and depression were my daily bread and butter. To cope, I overate, drank heavily, and relied on coffee and aspirin to get me through many a day. I was like a punch-drunk fighter, flailing away at my work, out of touch with my feelings or my body. It never occurred to me to relate my headaches and depression to what was happening in my marriage, my work or my personal life. Even though I felt just awful much of the time, I thought I was doing what was demanded of every committed Christian. My former parishioners can still picture me walking over to the parish from the parsonage with drooping shoulders and a despondent look.

Today, things are different, to be sure, but I still have difficulty managing the work and responsibility I undertake. I consistently live near the edge of my threshold level. If I misjudge this edge, as I frequently do, I experience specific physical manifestations of stress, like those heart palpitations a few months ago. What's different now is that I'm more aware of where the edge is for me and I know ways to pull myself back from the edge. In my self-care, I engage a wide variety of experts as consultants.

For example, each year I get a physical that includes tests of my cholesterol level and the ratio between my high density lipo-proteins and my low density lipo-proteins. As a middle-aged man, it's important to have my prostate checked annually. A cardiologist monitors my cardio-vascular system periodically, and I confer with another doctor about sports-related injuries. I see a psychologist when I'm showing signs of depression.

Four other persons are part of my health support system: an acupuncturist, whom I haven't seen for three years; my spiritual director with whom I've been meeting once a month for the past eight years, and a therapist couple whom Carole and I see when marital issues keep us from having fun.

Does this seem excessive or overindulgent? I don't believe it is. If staying healthy—physically, emotionally, and spiritually—is key to my effectiveness and credibility, then it's a professional expense I can't live without. Given that the medical professional deals primarily with pathology, not prevention, I've had to become my own medical expert, calling on a variety of specialists to help with specific areas of my life. I feel that how I manage stress is every bit as important as the research and insight I bring to my ministry. I invite you on to a similar path. Effective stress management will not only lengthen your life, but increase its quality as well.

There is one caveat. One doesn't enrich one's physical, emotional, and spiritual life without some effort and some pain. There will be self-perceptions to be examined, illusions to be shattered, conflicts, heretofore avoided, to be confronted. There will be tough disciplines to be learned and mastered and expectations that others have of you to be renegotiated. The driving force behind all the work must be a determination to gain control of your life and live it in a more wholistic, healthy fashion. Those around you will benefit in the long run, but at first they may not like it. It is my hope that the barriers between your current state and a healthier you will not seem insurmountable.

CHAPTER 4

Finding Out Where Your Edge Is: Stress Self-Assessment Tools

As we saw in the previous chapter, protecting oneself from too much stress requires a rather radical degree of self-knowledge, including a sensitivity to what your emotions, mind, and body are trying to tell you. Each of the several self-assessment tools included here looks at your level of stress from a different angle. Each individual's tolerance for stress varies, so these scales should be used as a rough guide. I hope that, taken together, the measures will help you get a handle on the particular areas that need some specific self-care.

Life Changes Rating Scales

The two scales that follow are based on an assessment tool developed by Dr. T.H. Holmes and Dr. R.H. Rahe.[1] Their basic premise, proven correct in four separate research efforts, is that the greater the number of social adjustments individuals make, the greater their potential for physical illness. I have taken the basic scale and adapted it for clergy and clergy spouses. Choose the scale that fits you. For each of the events that you have experienced in the last twelve months, transfer the Average Value to the line in Your Score column. When you are finished, add the numbers in Your Score column to get Your Total.

LIFE CHANGES FOR CLERGY

Event	Average Value	Your Score
Death of spouse	100	_____
Divorce	73	_____
Marital separation	65	_____
Death of close family member	63	_____
Personal injury or illness	53	_____
Marriage	50	_____
Serious decline in church attendance	49	_____
Geographical relocation	49	_____
Private meetings by segment of congregation to discuss your resignation	47	_____
Beginning of heavy drinking by immediate family member	46	_____
Marital reconciliation	45	
Retirement	45	_____
Change in health of a family member	44	_____
Problem with children	42	_____
Pregnancy	40	_____
Sex difficulties	39	_____
Alienation from one's Board/Council/Session/Vestry	39	_____
Gain of new family member	39	_____
New job in new line of work	38	_____
Change of financial state	38	_____
Death of close friend	37	_____
Increased arguing with spouse	35	_____
Merger of two or more congregations	35	_____
Serious parish financial difficulty	32	_____
Mortgage over $50,000 for home	31	_____
Difficulty with member of church staff (associates, organist, choir director, secretary, janitor, etc.)	31	_____
Foreclosure of mortgage or loan	30	_____
Destruction of church by fire	30	_____
New job in same line of work	30	_____
Son or daughter leaving home	29	_____
Trouble with in-laws	29	_____

Anger of influential church member over pastor action	29	_____
Slow steady decline in church attendance	29	_____
Outstanding personal achievement	28	_____
Introduction of new hymnal to worship service	28	_____
Failure of church to make payroll	27	_____
Remodeling or building program	27	_____
Start or stop of spouse's employment	26	_____
Holiday away	26	_____
Start or finish of school	26	_____
Death of peer	26	_____
Offer of call to another parish	26	_____
Change in living conditions	25	_____
Revision of personal habits	24	_____
Negative parish activity by former pastor	24	_____
Difficulty with confirmation class	22	_____
Change in residence	20	_____
Change in schools	20	_____
Change in recreation	19	_____
Change in social activities	18	_____
Death/moving away of good church leader	18	_____
Mortgage or personal loan of less than $50,000	17	_____
Change in sleeping habits	16	_____
Developing of new friendships	16	_____
Change in eating habits	15	_____
Stressful continuing education experience	15	_____
Major program change	15	_____
Vacation at home	13	_____
Christmas	12	_____
Lent	12	_____
Easter	12	_____
Minor violation of the law	11	_____

Your Total _____

LIFE CHANGES FOR CLERGY SPOUSES

Event	Average Value	Your Score
Death of spouse	100	
Divorce/break up of family	73	_____
Loss of job/setback in your career	70	_____
Serious communication problem with spouse	69	_____
Marital separation	65	_____
Unwanted pregnancy	65	_____
Death of immediate family member	65	_____
Personal injury or illness	63	_____
Unemployment of spouse	60	_____
Being physically abused by your spouse	59	_____
Immediate family member attempts suicide	55	_____
Getting into debt beyond means of repayment	51	_____
Beginning of heavy drinking by immediate family member	46	_____
Marital reconciliation	45	_____
Retirement	45	_____
Change of lifestyle; move to new community	43	_____
Pregnancy	40	_____
Miscarriage	40	_____
Difficulties in sexual relationship	39	_____
Serious illness or injury requires hospitalization	39	_____
New job in new line of work	38	_____
Change in financial state	38	_____
Death of close friend	37	_____
Increased arguments with spouse	37	_____
Severing intimate relationship/friendship	35	_____
Abortion (voluntarily induced)	32	_____
Immediate family member sent to jail	32	_____
Divorce within extended family	32	_____
Purchase of house, mortgage over $100,000	31	_____
New problem related to use of alcohol or drugs	30	_____
Foreclosure of mortgage or loan	30	_____
Spouse begins or stops work	30	_____
Immediate family member seriously ill	30	_____
Son or daughter leaving home	29	_____

Beginning a new friendship/relationship	29	_____
Trouble with in-laws	29	_____
Outstanding personal achievement	28	_____
Conflict with close friend	27	_____
Holiday away	26	_____
Serious restriction of social life	25	_____
Problem with children	24	_____
Onset of prolonged ill health requiring doctor's treatment	23	_____
Increase in family arguments	22	_____
Addition of new resident in the home	21	_____
Moving to new house	20	_____
Demanding relationship outside nuclear family	18	_____
Spouse introduces stresses from job to home	18	_____
Single parenting/spouse unavailable	17	_____
New job in same line of work	17	_____
Remodeling of home	16	_____
Development of new friendship	16	_____
Build up of tedious household chores	15	_____
No privacy in living arrangements	15	_____
Change in sleeping habits	15	_____
Change in appetite/eating habits	15	_____
Vacation at home	15	_____
Christmas	12	_____
Lent	12	_____
Easter	12	_____
Minor violation of law	11	_____

Your Total _____

Adapted by Roy M. Oswald and Linda Kramer from the Holmes/Rahe Life Changes Rating Scale.

Scoring the Survey

The survey you have just taken is an excellent reminder of all the life
transitions you have gone though in the past twelve months. Perhaps you
have been bombarded lately with a number of major life changes. No
wonder you feel tired and depressed!

The following will give you a sense of your score in relation to other
clergy or clergy spouses:

50 or below	unusually low
51-100	stress very manageable
101-150	stress moderately manageable
151-200	borderline—mild concern appropriate
201-250	mildly serious
251-300	moderately serious
301-350	very serious
351 and above	alarming

Holmes and Rahe, in several key experiments with their scale, discovered that those in the top one third in numbers of social readjustments
during one year had ninety percent more illnesses than the lower two
thirds.

This research teaches something very important about myself and all
other human beings on the planet: We simply do not have limitless
ability to adjust to change around us. Too many changes make us sick.
If they continue unabated they will eventually kill us. This is part of
what it means to be a finite human being.

Years ago Alvin Toffler predicted this phenomenon in his book,
Future Shock.[2] He described future shock as the future coming in on us
at such a rate that we are not able to adjust. The result: the organism
breaks down. We get sick. In extreme cases, we die. Being out of
control seems to be a key contributor to deadly stress. Two studies
conducted in 1972 by Parkes and Jenkins indicated that people who had
recently lost a loved one or had lost a job had a higher than average rate
of illness and death.[3,4] Medical research also reports situations in which
individuals died within minutes or hours of a significant and stressful life
event. Two fundamental factors in the onset of illness or sudden death
have been described as "fruitless struggle" and "giving up."

Among animals and humans, the inability to predict and maintain a degree of control over our environment, or the inability to garner support for ourselves when under stress, contributes greatly to a swing from health to illness, from life to death. In 1965, social scientist George L. Engel collected newspaper clippings of 275 cases of sudden death and placed them in four categories: 1) 135 deaths were related to a traumatic event in a close human relationship; 2) 103 deaths involved situations of danger, struggle, or attack; 3) 21 deaths involved loss of status, humiliation, failure, or defeat (all were men); and 4) 16 deaths occurred at moments of great triumph or personal joy.[5]

The last category is worth noting because it points to the truth that our bodies often cannot tell the difference between a positive stress and a negative one: e.g., getting married versus being fired from a job. Both require of us massive readjustments that can put us way over our threshold level of stress. Two noteworthy examples of sudden death relate to this dichotomy: A fifty-six-year-old minister was so elated that he would have a chance to speak to President Carter that he suffered a fatal heart attack. Lyndon B. Johnson suffered his fatal heart attack the day after the newly inaugurated Richard M. Nixon announced the dismantling of many of the Great Society programs.

Each of us is unique in how we respond to life-changing events. Some people have high adventure needs along with a certain psychological hardiness that allow them to endure scores of 500 or more on the stress scale without a hint of illness. Others are thrown off balance by relatively minor changes in their routine; scores as low as 150 to 200 may push then beyond their threshold. For each of us there comes a point where the adjustments we are having to make no longer press us to greater creativity, but become toxic to our lives. While the life changes scale cannot predict illness, it can help locate the experiences that push you near your threshold.

THE STRAIN RESPONSE

This self-assessment tool is, for me, the most important one. It measures only the physical and psychological indicators of stress. Once you have completed it, we will relate this score to your other scores.

0 = Never
1 = Infrequently
2 = Frequently
3 = Regularly

_____ 1. Eat too much
_____ 2. Drink too much alcohol
_____ 3. Smoke more than usual
_____ 4. Feel tense, uptight, fidgety
_____ 5. Feel depressed or remorseful
_____ 6. Like myself less
_____ 7. Have difficulty going to sleep or staying asleep
_____ 8. Feel restless and unable to concentrate
_____ 9. Have decreased interest in sex
_____ 10. Have increased interest in sex
_____ 11. Have loss of appetite
_____ 12. Feel tired/low energy
_____ 13. Feel irritable
_____ 14. Think about suicide
_____ 15. Become less communicative
_____ 16. Feel disoriented or overwhelmed
_____ 17. Have difficulty getting up in the morning
_____ 18. Have headaches
_____ 19. Have upset stomach
_____ 20. Have sweaty and/or trembling hands
_____ 21. Have shortness of breath and sighing
_____ 22. Let things slide
_____ 23. Misdirect anger
_____ 24. Feel "unhealthy"
_____ 25. Feel time-bound, anxious about too much to do in too little time
_____ 26. Use prescription drugs to relax
_____ 27. Use medication for high blood pressure
_____ 28. Depend on recreational drugs to relax
_____ 29. Have anxiety about the future

_____ 30. Have back problems

_____ 31. Unable to clear up a cold, running nose, sore throat, cough, infection, etc.

_____ **Your Total Score**

0-20	Below average strain in your life
21-30	Stress starting to show its effects in your life. You are living near your stress threshold, at times crossing it.
31-40	Above average strain. Stress is have a very destructive effect on your life. You are living a good portion of your life beyond your stress threshold.
Above 40	Unless you do something soon to alleviate your stress, more serious illness will follow.

Adapted from John D. Adams' survey, "The Strain Response." Used by permission.

_____

I invite you now to place your two survey scores together on this page.

Life Changes _____
The Strain Response _____

If your strain response score is above twenty-five, try to pinpoint the specific areas that produce the greatest stress for you. What are the things that give you headaches or upset stomachs? With specific stressors in mind, you can develop specific strategies to counteract their destructive impact.

CHAPTER 5

Crossing the Stress Threshold

When you are above your threshold level of stress you are a disaster waiting to happen. It's not merely bad luck that you had a heart attack or some other illness. In many cases, disease strikes an unhealthy body. Many medical scientists now believe that all disease has both a biological and a psychosocial component; some research indicates that the psychosocial component may be the more powerful of the two.[1]

How do we know when we have surpassed our threshold level of stress? First, we need to get back in touch with our body and begin listening to the messages it is sending us. The disciplines of meditation, centering, and journaling can help us in this regard. Fifteen years ago I would have dismissed the idea that I was out of touch with my body. After all, I was living in my body. How could I not be aware of what it was telling me? But the truth is, I was often unaware until my body practically shouted at me with excruciating migraines or severe stomach pains.

A chart and an illustration will help us understand our stress threshold better.

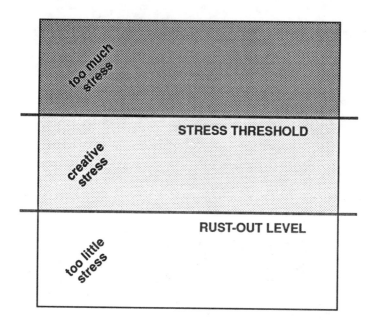

Please note the rust-out level. There is such a thing as having so little stress in one's life that one loses interest and dies. I think this often happens to older adults in certain homes for the aging when, in the name of caring, every significant decision is taken away from them. All of us need a little stress to keep us stimulated and alive, to get us out of bed in the morning.

Studies of the relationship between creativity and stress conducted at the University of Ontario in London, Ontario, confirm that creativity decreases when we go below our rust-out level or above our threshold level. When I was a parish pastor, I usually prepared my sermon on Saturday night (I was rarely organized enough to get much done earlier in the week). Generally, my sermons were fairly creative–unless, of course, I was hit with a crisis or two on Saturday that drained away my energy. On those occasions, I had no creative juice left, and I had to borrow someone else's spirituality by stealing a sermon from a book. I was clearly over my stress threshold level.

Sample of how one pastor exceeded his Stress Threshold

>	His most trusted lay leader got transferred to another city.
<	He began a heavy round of parish home visits.
<	He agreed to write a devotional booklet for his denomination.
<	He and his spouse took the trip to Greece they have been planning for years.

Stress

Threshold

>	Several powerful lay leaders thought it was time he left.
>	A close clergy colleague died.
>	His oldest son left for college.
>	An automobile accident left him with a severely brused knee.
>	The congregation voted a renovation program for the sanctuary.
>	The IRS asked to audit his last year's income tax statement.
<	He was elected chairperson of the local ministerial association.
>	The church was broken into and slightly vandalized.
>	His adolescent daughter began dating and staying out late.
<	He joined the YMCA to begin an exercise program.
>	His doctor advised bifocals.
<	He began a Doctor of Ministry program at a nearby seminary.

Stress

Threshold

Key		
	>	Events not in your control.
	<	Events in your control.

As you can see, the majority of transitions in this pastor's life are out of his control. So he must work with those areas of flux over which he has some control. Effective stress management is a little like piloting a sailboat when a flash storm arises. You can't do anything to prevent the storm, but you can exercise some control over the boat, such as pulling down the sail, starting the engines, clearing the deck, or putting on a raincoat. (Of course, the clergy person is not the only one in that boat. If he or she is married or in a significant relationship, another is dealing with the storms, too, and the stresses are different for each. See the chart, "Stress in Ministry: It's a Family Affair," on the following page).

"Today you've chaired three committee meetings, attended two potluck dinners, opened the bazaar, and refereed a boys' basketball game . . . how could you feel 'unfulfilled'?"

STRESS IN MINISTRY: IT'S A FAMILY AFFAIR

In fifteen years of workshops with clergy and their spouses, the following issues have been listed as most stressful. This list includes the key stressors for clergy spouses. (For the most part, these apply more to clergy wives than clergy husbands. Congregations have had centuries of experience with clergy wives and thus tend to have more unconscious projections onto women in this role.)

CLERGY

Role Ambiguity—When pastors have an unclear picture of their role they work harder to cover all the bases.

Role Conflict—Pastoral expectations often conflict with personal or family expectations.

Role Overload—Pastors become overwhelmed by all the expectations of parishioners.

Time Demands—Clergy are on call twenty-four hours a day, seven days a week, making planning difficult.

Lack of Pastoral Care—Most clergy do not have a good mentor or solid spiritual advisors/counselors/friends.

Lack of Opportunities for Extra-Dependence—Clergy need opportunities to de-role and be taken care of.

Geographical Relocation—When you move, almost everything changes, requiring massive readjustments.

Political/Economic Uncertainty—Much of your political/economic/career future depends on your relationship with a particular parish.

A Helping Profession—Those in the helping professions burn out more often than other professionals.

Loneliness—Beyond fellow clergy, very few persons understand the role of parish pastor or the demands of pastoral work. Hence, the feeling of loneliness and isolation.

SPOUSE

Role Expectations—Parishioners have certain ideas about how the minister's spouse should behave.

Surrogate Clergy—When the ordained person is unavailable, lay persons sometimes unload their anxiety on the available spouse.

Super Person—The person married to the minister often manages several roles: employee outside the home, manager of the homefront, and other roles within the church.

Lack of Pastoral Care—One cannot be lover, husband/wife, and pastor to the same person. If you are not pastor to your spouse, who is?

Geographical Relocation—Clergy spouses are often affected more negatively by a move than clergy. Clergy have a more clearly defined role and get involved immediately; it's more difficult for a spouse to find his/her way.

Lack of Support—Support for the spouse in the parish may be inadequate.

Parsonage Living—When your home belongs to the parish, how you use the home may be scrutinized.

Finances—Because of low pastor salaries, many spouses are forced to seek employment even when they have small children at home.

What Happens When You Cross Your Stress Threshold

Stress management can be defined as living our lives somewhere between the extremes of rust-out at the bottom and blow-out at the top. If
we fail to manage our stress, the stress will manage us, eventually ren-
dering us dysfunctional in our pastoral role. (The case of Susan Miller in
the introduction illustrates this phenomenon.)

When we consistently exceed our stress threshold, we lose our capacity to function at optimum levels. Some of the effects are:

1. Decrease in Perception

Under normal circumstances we can take in from our environment all the
data we need to function well. Under prolonged stress, the amount of
data we can process diminishes. Most of us know the effects of those
extra-full days: we conduct two or three services Sunday morning,
attend a parish event all afternoon and another engagement in the evening. By Sunday evening we realize we are only hearing a fraction of
the conversations being directed our way. It's like overloading a computer. The screen flashes, "Data Overload Error—Cannot Save This
Page." I can recall several times when I knew people's words were not
penetrating my brain. I was simply overloaded; I couldn't retain anything else.

2. Perceived Loss of Options

When we cross our stress threshold, we cannot see clearly all the options
available to us. At times like these, our friends can be very important to
us because they can often see alternatives that we cannot.

The ability to see options is one of the most valuable things we can
offer parishioners when tragedy strikes their lives. They will often see
few ways out of their situation—and bad ways at that. We can help
expand their vision if we ourselves are in a good place where stress is not
overwhelming us.

3. Regression to Infantile Behavior

When we're excessively stressed, we tend to revert to old, familiar behavior patterns. At such times it's important to remember how we reacted to stress as a child and identify those behaviors that, if acted out while in the role of clergyperson, would jeopardize our credibility.

In my first parish, I counseled a female parishioner over the course of two years. Naive as I was, I didn't realize anything was amiss until one day she made a pass at me. I extricated myself from the scene, drove home, and crawled into bed with my clothes on. I can still see myself in a fetal position under the bedcovers.

Another time I got so angry at a professional colleague that I ripped off a letter on my typewriter at two in the morning and dropped it in the mailbox before I went back to sleep. The next day I wished more than anything to get my letter back. Fortunately, the colleague and I remained friends. He jokes about having the letter framed for me one day. Other times when I have responded in anger have not been redeemable. I have hurt myself professionally by regressing to infantile behavior in times of stress.

4. Inability to Make Changes in Destructive Relationship Patterns

When our lives are in stress we may find it difficult to extricate ourselves from relationships that are toxic to us. I'm much less able to confront someone when I'm under excessive stress because that would mean making changes, and I simply can't introduce more stress to my life. When people make unreasonable demands on me, I find it easier to say "yes" than to hold my ground. I take on more work because I simply don't have the emotional energy to say "no."

5. Fatigue

When we are under excessive stress we need more rest and sleep than usual. In our Clergy in Transition seminars, we encourage participants to give themselves permission to rest more while they make their move into a new job and role.

The confusion and self-doubt that occur in times of stress are often debilitating. We wonder if we are losing our capacity to cope or are simply getting too old. This self-doubt is misdirected. When we grant ourselves the right to rest more during times of transition, our vitality will return once we're through the crisis time.

6. Depression

Depression often strikes those who cross the stress threshold. Change of
any kind involves loss and we have to allow ourselves to grieve. Even
when we've made a positive transition, we will miss some of our former
roles or identities. The grieving may be at an unconscious level.

Most of us have trouble dealing with loss; some of us find grief
work more difficult than others. Yet even the toughest among us will
probably experience some crankiness and irritability or simply "blue"
feelings when our predictable world disappears and we must deal with a
new one.

7. Physical Illness

When we consistently pump adrenaline into our system, the physiological action tends to affect the weakest link in our genetic code first. This
is one reason medical personnel delve into our medical history to find out
what diseases pop up often in our families of origin.

People often experience the effects of stress in one of these four
categories:

a. Cardiovascular System: heart disease, high blood pressure,
strokes, respiratory illnesses.

b. Gastronomical System: ulcer, colitis, hemorrhoids, acid stomach.

c. Structural/Skeletal System: back and neck pains, diseases of the
joints and bones.

d. Immune System: colds, flu, or other communicable diseases.[2]

The phrase "catching a cold" can be a misnomer. We may give ourselves a cold by allowing stress to lower our resistance. We may notice
that even though all family members are exposed to a cold virus, only the
most stressed-out members catch the cold.

There are only two healthy ways to respond when you exceed your
threshold level:

1. You can simplify your life by changing those areas over which
you have some control.

2. Through radical self-care stategies, you can raise your threshold

level so you can handle more stress. (We will consider some of these strategies later in the book.)

You probably have tried both of the above at various times to varying degrees. When my heart starts to palpitate, I know I need to ease up on my commitments. Sometimes I let my friends and family members down by excusing myself from social functions. Trying to simplify my life is rarely a guilt-free process. If I cancel a contract or two, I feel the loss of credibility and reputation with my clients. It doesn't feel good, yet in the long run I know it is the wise decision.

In the next chapter we'll look at one pastor who crossed her stress threshold, but managed to fight her way back to relative health again.

CHAPTER 6

Returning from the Brink: Susan Miller's Story

When we last visited Susan Miller in the introduction, she was knee-deep in trouble after two years in her new church, and the waters were rising. She was suffering back and stomach problems clearly related to many stresses that had converged on her all at once: a divorce, a cross-country move away from family, friends, and other support networks, and a new job and a new town to adjust to. And these stresses were on top of the normal stress that comes with being a resident religious authority in a church community.

Yet, despite the sure signs that things were not well, Susan might have continued slogging along—if she had not encountered a severe medical crisis.

The day after Easter, Susan entered the hospital with a bleeding ulcer. It was then that several clergywomen in Susan's new synod came to talk turkey. They had been watching the results of her inability to handle stress, and they were worried, not only for Susan personally, but also for the image that was being projected within the synod that women couldn't handle larger parishes.

In the course of that initial bedside meeting, four of the clergy-women agreed to meet for half a day every two weeks to support each other in dealing with the stress of their ministries. One of the women even committed to driving two hours one way to make the meetings, and the others gave the support group equally high priority. Meeting at a nearby hospital where one of the women was chaplain, the women found the group to be an oasis of support, a place to laugh about the politics within their congregations and the synod, a safe haven for letting the lid off the pressure cooker for a bit.

Once Susan's ulcer was under control, her doctor recommended that she begin treatment in relaxation and biofeedback at a local clinic. Susan began using the relaxation techniques each morning and evening for twenty minutes, and the biofeedback mechanisms allowed her to actually lower her stress level. Later Susan began seeing a spiritual director and learned a process of meditation that combined prayer with relaxation.

Things at Holy Comforter, however, continued to keep Susan off balance. At the end of her first year in the parish, with the support of the church council, Susan had shifted the time of the Sunday school classes, which used to run concurrently with the 9:30 worship service. She had thought there was solid support for committing an hour to study and an hour to worship on Sunday morning. Both Susan and the council had underestimated the resistance to this rescheduling. Several families left the church over it. Attendance at the 9:00 a.m. service dropped ten percent, and the children's Sunday school enrollment dropped by twelve percent. By the end of that year, giving was down fifteen percent.

It was hard for Susan not to take it personally. As the pressure hit, she began to let her meditation times slip to only once a day. But even that, plus her support group, helped her stay on her feet.

During this tense period, a long-term pastor in the same city turned out to be a real support to Susan. He had noticed for years how Holy Comforter tended to be hard on its pastors. He suggested that Susan set up a pastor/parish relations committee with two foci. First, it would serve as support and advocate for Susan's self-care. Second, it would help her to gain a clearer perception of what the congregation needed and wanted from her as pastor. Susan acted on this suggestion and chose people she felt she could trust and depend on.

It took the group six months to gain perspective on the demands being placed on Susan, but when it did its first recommendation was that Susan take two days off per week and limit herself to fifty hours of work a week. Susan knew she needed that amount of time to rest and make connections with friends and family members, but her anxiety about doing well in the parish and keeping everyone reasonably satisfied made it hard for her to take even one day off per week. The group gently cajoled her into taking more time for herself: "The church needs that kind of stability and consistency from you," they argued, and after a while Susan began to trust their perceptions. On her days off, Susan took time to drive to a nearby city to be with friends. Occasionally she flew back East to visit her daughter.

By the end of her fourth year in the parish, Susan began to feel her vitality returning. Some younger families began attending Sunday worship, and attendance at Sunday School increased. This appeared to ease some of the tension in the parish over Susan's ministry. Finally, contributions began to rise, too.

One afternoon while at her synod's office, Susan ran into the bishop in the hall. "How are things going at Holy Comforter?" he asked. Susan replied, "I'm having a ball," and for the first time, she meant it.

Returning from the brink of stress city can be scary. While in the middle of the confusion and pain, it sometimes feels as though the whole bundle is going to come unravelled. A seminary classmate of mine, four years into his first parish, had what was called a "nervous breakdown." It was not a pleasant sight. He had to take a six-month leave of absence to get his life back together again. He was and is a beautiful person, and I'm glad to report that he has survived and remains in the parish ministry.

There is hope for each of us in managing the stress of our lives. In Part Four we will consider more self-care strategies that helped to many ministers. But before that, let's consider the second twin destroyer— burnout. Burnout is quite different from stress, although the symptoms and causes may look the same. In the next section, we will attempt to tease out the subtle difference between the two.

PART THREE

Burnout and the Ministry

CHAPTER 7

When the Salt Loses Its Savor

I was looking forward to seeing my old friend Bill Miller, pastor of a 1,200-member downtown church in a major metropolitan area.* Though we had known each other for over a decade, Bill and I had gotten together only infrequently during the five years he had been at First Church. I was glad that one of my seminars had finally landed me in town so I could have dinner with Bill and his wife, Harriet.

It didn't take long to realize that something had gone awry in Bill's life. He was heavier than I remembered and smoking cigarettes at a faster pace than I had seen before. Most of our dinner conversation focused on Bill. He just wasn't having fun being a pastor anymore. He felt his parish was demanding his last bucket of blood. He had been away for six weeks of continuing education and then a vacation in August and yet by November he was wondering if he could make it until his next vacation.

"When do you take time off from the parish?" I asked.

"Technically, Saturday is supposed to be my day off," he said, "but every time there's a wedding, I need to sacrifice that time. I bet I've married seventy-five couples in the five years I've been here."

"And Saturday night is sermon writing time," Harriet chimed in.

In a flash I got a picture of Bill's life: except for vacations, he worked flat out six days a week, except for Saturday, which was pre-empted every few weeks by a wedding. Even when he did get a full Saturday off, there was still the sermon that needed to be prepared. I was

*Names and details have been changed.

wondering what was driving him so hard when Bill began talking about the "exodus" that had occured two years ago.

Bill had followed a pastor who had served First Church for twenty-eight years. The fact that Bill was very different from this former pastor caused dissatisfaction and tension in the parish. When forty families transferred out of the parish, Bill took it personally. True to the literature on burnout, Bill turned the sword inward, blamed himself for the incident and began trying harder. There was always this voice in his head: "Don't be your authentic self. Be like your predecessor." I happened to know that Bill's authentic self was quite delightful, so it really hurt to hear that he was repressing his best qualities to try to please this parish.

Bill did admit that some good things were happening. In spite of membership losses, giving had continued to rise, and there was a new sense of vitality in Sunday worship. Yet the kick in the stomach, the thing that drove Bill to work almost nonstop, was his sense of failure over not being Superman and making everyone happy (part of his irrational belief system that we will talk about later.)

Bill's anger was close to the surface. "You know what really gets me," he said, "When people in the parish come up to me and say, 'Did you know that so-and-so has not been in church for the last three weeks and that no one has dropped by to see him?'" Bill pounded the table, "At this point I really want to say, 'Hey, why don't you GROW UP? When are we going to stop playing games meant for three-year-olds? If you're so concerned, why don't you go and see them and find out where their fragile egos have been bruised?'

"And then there are the ones who constantly remind me of all the little things that are wrong around here or that aren't being done, or done their way," Bill continued. "It would be different if it were an all-out conflict situation. But how do you keep loving folks when they are kicking you in the shins half the time?"

"You know when I notice it the most," Harriet added. "It's when he comes home at night and doesn't want to do a thing. He doesn't want to talk with me or Jill (their daughter). He just wants to be left alone."

"He's over-peopled," I responded. "He's been bombarded with people's concerns all day; he doesn't have the emotional energy to deal with one more person." Knowing Bill was an Introvert and Harriet an Extravert[1], I suspected there was some tension between them about Bill not engaging in conversation, about sharing his day when he got home.

Bill loves to read. He confessed to going into a bookstore several times and buying two or three books he'd really like to read, then putting them on the shelf and never opening them. The congregation was missing an important part of Bill because parish work had pre-empted his reading time.

My heart was heavy with Bill and Harriet's plight. Here were two of my favorite people, and their lives were dry and joyless. Their hopeful and fun-loving approach to life had evaporated in the heat of a parish's never-ending demands.

When I shared with Bill my conviction that clergy need to strive to do their ministry in fifty hours a week or less—and also take two days off per week like everyone else—he looked stunned. I asked him if he thought his session would resist him in this discipline. He said no. It had just never occurred to him to ask. Of course, Bill would need a lot more than that to regain his vitality, but it was a start.

Bill stayed on at First Church another four years. When I dropped in to see him just prior to his resignation he told me he and Harriet were going to sell their house and buy a small cabin in the Ozarks. Both of them would work odd jobs to pay their expenses. It was pretty radical, but I knew this was what Bill needed to do to regain his soul.

That was five years ago. Bill now says he's ready to take on another parish. At fifty-five, with his vitality back, Bill will probably make some church a superior pastor. Unfortunately, the church does not support people who care for themselves in dramatic ways as Bill did. Church executives and search committees are reluctant even to look at the dossier of a person who has been out of the active ministry for a time. I'm confident, however, that some parish out there will interview Bill and be struck by his depth and vitality.

What Is Burnout?

Burnout of the kind Bill suffered is often thought to be the result of chronic stress. When a person remains in a stressful situation over an extended period, s/he burns out. Yet from another perspective, stress and burnout are quite different animals. With stress, too much change or novelty forces people to overuse their adjustment capacities and, after awhile, they become either physically or emotionally ill. Burnout can occur when people overuse their listening or caring capacities. They become consumed by too many needy people or too much responsibility over long periods of time.

THE DIFFERENCES BETWEEN STRESS AND BURNOUT

Stress and burnout deplete one's body and soul in distinct ways. Stress taxes our adjustment capacities, while burnout taxes our ability to continuing caring.

STRESS involves...

Overuse of our adjustment capacities.
Too much transition, novelty, change.

Resulting in...

Loss of perception
Loss of options
Regression to infantile behavior
Being locked into destructive relationships
Fatigue
Depression
Physical illness

BURNOUT involves...

Overuse of our listening and caring capacities
Too many needy people
Too much responsibility

Resulting in...

Physical and emotional exhaustion
Cynicism
Disillusionment
Self-Depreciation

Psychoanalyst Herbert Freudenberger, author of *Burnout: The High Cost of High Achievement,* describes burnout as "a state of fatigue or frustration brought about by devotion to a cause, way of life, or relationship that failed to produce the expected reward."[2] Jerry Edelwich and Archie Brodsky, in their book, *Burnout,* define it as a "progressive loss of idealism, energy, and purpose experienced by people in the helping professions."[3] Psychologist Christine Maslach at the University of California at Berkeley defines burnout as "a state of physical, emotional and mental exhaustion marked by physical depletion and chronic fatique, feelings of helplessness and hopelessness, and by development of negative self-concept and negative attitudes towards work, life and other people."[4]

What do the definitions of burnout have in common?

- Decreased energy—physically, the individual has difficulty keeping up the pace.
- Decreased self-esteem—the individual feels a sense of personal failure related to work or vocation.
- Output exceeding input—the person has poured more and more of him/herself into a job or project, and the expected payoff or rewards are not forthcoming.
- Sense of helplessness, hopelessness, being trapped—the individual is unable to perceive alternate ways of functioning.
- Loss of idealism—the individual's worldview has been shattered.
- Cynicism and negativism—the individual is down on self, others, the job, institutions, etc.
- Self-depletion—the individual's resources to continue seem to be diminishing.

Looking at burnout from a wholistic perspective, this malaise touches us at four levels:

Biologically—specific physical symptoms appear.

Psychologically—our emotional make-up is measurably altered.

Sociologically—a dysfunctional relationship exists between ourselves and our work, and possibly between our family and our church as well.

Spiritually—our worldview or view of reality is significantly altered.

Burnout is a pervasive disease touching all aspects of a person's life. As such, it needs to be treated at all four levels to achieve health and wholeness.

Before looking more deeply at the phenomenon of burnout, let's determine where we are in the burn-out cycle. The next chapter offers an instrument that has proven effective in measuring clergy burn-out levels.

CHAPTER 8

How Dry Is Your Well?
A Burnout Self-Assessment Tool

Over the past ten years the following clergy burn-out rating scale has been revised several times. It's a simple inventory, and I am consistently amazed at how accurately it identifies those experiencing, or on their way to, burnout. I invite you to rate yourself.

CLERGY BURN-OUT INVENTORY(CBI)
Developed by Roy M. Oswald, The Alban Institute, Inc.

For each question, circle the number from 1 to 6 that best describes you. Then add all your answers for your total score.

1. The extent to which I am feeling negative or cynical about the people with whom I work (despairing of their ability to change and grow)

	1	2	3	4	5	6

Optimistic
about parishioners

Cynical about
parishioners

2. The extent to which I have enthusiasm for my work (I enjoy my work and look foward to it regularly.)

	1	2	3	4	5	6

High internal
energy for my
work

Loss of enthu-
siasm for my
job

3. The extent to which I invest myself emotionally in my work in the parish

1	2	3	4	5	6
Highly invested					Withdrawn and
emotionally					detached

4. The extent to which fatigue and irritation are part of my daily experience

1	2	3	4	5	6
Cheerfulness,					Tired and
high energy					irritated much
much of the time					of the time

5. The extent to which my humor has a cynical, biting tone

1	2	3	4	5	6
Humor reflects a					Humor cynical
a positive joyful					and sarcastic
attitude					

6. The extent to which I find myself spending less and less time with my parishioners

1	2	3	4	5	6
Eager to be					Increasing with-
involved with					drawal from
parishioners					parishioners

7. The extent to which I am becoming less flexible in my dealings with parishioners

1	2	3	4	5	6
Remaining open					Becoming more
and flexible with					fixed and rigid
parishioners' needs					in dealing with
and wants					parishioners

8. The extent to which I feel supported in my work

1	2	3	4	5	6
Feeling fully supported					Feeling alone and isolated

9. The extent to which I find myself frustrated in my attempts to accomplish tasks important to me

1	2	3	4	5	6
Reasonably successful in accomplishing tasks					Mainly frustrated in accomplished tasks

10. The extent to which I am invaded by sadness I can't explain

1	2	3	4	5	6
Generally optimistic					Sad much of the time

11. The extent to which I am suffering from physical complaints (e.g., aches, pains, headaches, lingering colds, etc.)

1	2	3	4	5	6
Feeling healthy most of the time					Constantly irritated by physical ailments

12. The extent to which sexual activity seems more trouble than it is worth

1	2	3	4	5	6
Sex is a high					Sexual activity is just another responsibility

13. The extent to which I blame others for problems I encounter

1	2	3	4	5	6
Minimal blaming or scapegoating					Others are usually to blame for the malaise I'm feeling

14. The extent to which I feel guilty about what is not happening in this parish or with parishioners

1	2	3	4	5	6
Guilt free					Feeling guilty much of the time

15. The extent to which I am biding my time until retirement or a change of job

1	2	3	4	5	6
Highly engaged in my work					Doing what I have to to get by

16. The extent to which I feel used up and spent

1	2	3	4	5	6
High source of energy for my work					Feeling empty and depleted

Total of numbers circled _____

0-32	Burnout not an issue
33-48	Bordering on burnout
49-64	Burnout a factor in my life
65-80	You are a victim of extreme burnout. Your life needs a radical change so you can regain your health and vitality.

Before going on, take a minute to fully absorb the meaning of your total score. If you have a score of forty or less, burnout is not really a factor in your life and ministry. If your stress and strain scores are of concern to you, you may want to focus more on the self-care strategies that deal with stress.

If you have a score of fifty or more, I recommend that you take seriously the impact that burnout is having on your ministry and primary relationships. The following reflection questions may help you focus:

1. Because burnout usually creeps up on us unaware, recall the times when you were not experiencing this condition. What changes took place in your life and/or work to help bring this about?

2. What are some options that could help to alleviate the symptoms of burnout?

3. Who are the individuals or resources you can turn to to help you reverse the burn-out trends in your life?

CHAPTER 9

The Disease
of the Overcommitted

Some of you may have been surprised at how you scored on the Burn-out Inventory in the last chapter. You knew you were feeling some pressure and that you don't have the zip you used to, but you didn't know the well was as dry as it is. Others of you are on the borderline of burnout, and if things don't change in the next few years, you'll probably arrive there. Many of you, I hope, are no where near burnout. You have a marvelous opportunity to use the self-care strategies in the last section of this book as preventive measures. How much better to be ahead of the crisis rather than trying to pick up the pieces after things fall apart.

Burnout seems to be the particular disease of those in the helping professions: social workers, teachers, nurses, police workers, poverty lawyers, therapists, physicians—and clergy. We could add parents to the list, especially parents in poor families with lots of kids. The key factor that determines whether people in these professions burn out seems to be *control*. How much control does the person have over how many needy, hurting people invade their space? Social workers, teachers, clergy, police, and parents have less control than those with regular office hours.

In my stress and burn-out seminars, one in five clergy scores high on the burnout rating scale. Among clergy who have been in their parish for ten years or more, the number doubles. These clergy still perform their pastoral functions with skill and concern, but they have lost their zest and vitality. They have become dull, hollow, and uninteresting, and they know it. The tragedy is that these are probably some of our most dedicated and committed clergy. They are not really dull and uncreative; they have simply given so much of themselves for so long that they are burned out.

Burnout among church professionals seems to be cyclical in nature, as the graphic below illustrates.

CLERGY BURN-OUT CYCLE

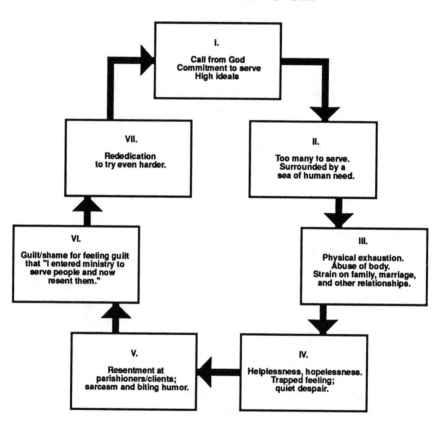

We clergy begin our ministries with high hopes and high energy. In our *enthusiasm* we may have unrealistic expectations and begin to over-identify with the job. This can lead to *stagnation*, a phase in which personal, financial, and career development needs begin to be felt. When we begin to question whether our efforts are worth anything, we become *frustrated.*

Frustration is a crossroad that can lead us back to enthusiasm (through a constructive rechanneling of energy). We may go through the cycle from enthusiasm to frustration many times in our careers. But frustration can also degenerate into *apathy*, an abyss of chronic indifference that defies most intervention. Frustration may enable us to learn how to cope with our limitations, but when we sink into apathy, we have fallen prey to burnout.

You're probably wondering what makes some people more susceptible to burnout than others. "Pastor Joe over there at Second Church never takes care of himself. He goes full steam all the time and never suffers any ill effects," you say. Most of us know these clergy. They're task-oriented, hard-working, and always exceed job expectations, yet it doesn't seem to affect them. We usually call these people workaholics. According to psychologist Marilyn Macholwitz, workaholics are compulsive workers who have a genuine love for work.[1] They may not be capable of relating to others in a deeply personal or intimate way, but they can and usually do succeed in going through their entire life without burning out. Perhaps their ability to use compulsive work as a defense mechanism protects them from getting emotionally close to people and experiencing the anxiety, frustrations, and stress felt by the more vulnerable individuals who do burn out.

Most of us, though, do not have the characteristics of workaholics. Our compulsive work habits don't protect us from burnout. In fact, they may contribute to it. Generally, the clergy people most susceptible to burnout:

— are idealistic and over-committed
— are in direct contact with the poor, the sick, and the dying where setbacks and discouragement are the order of the day
— have high needs to please everyone and a low tolerance for dissonance in the parish
— avoid conflict (When conflicts are rarely faced directly, the

minister has to double her/his efforts to keep things on an even
keel.)
— have difficulty saying "no" to protect personal boundaries or to
make time for rest, relationships, and recreation
— suffer from role confusion ("I don't quite know what people
expect of me in this role, so I'll just try to keep all bases covered
at all times.")

How Burnout Takes Its Toll

The chart "Differences Between Stress and Burnout" on page 58 listed
four of the most common results of burnout: physical and emotional
exhaus-tion, cynicism, disillusionment, and self-depreciation. Let's take
a closer look at them.

Physical and Emotional Exhaustion. We all know what physical
exhaustion feels like. We crave a few days off or a good night's sleep.
Emotional exhaustion is something different. It's that sinking feeling
inside that has you wondering if you have another stewardship drive left
in you. It's that strong feeling that you just can't handle another meeting
this evening, or the sense that the last thing you want to do is stand up in
front of another group of people.

Cynicism. Even worse than the exhaustion is the growing negative feeling you have about your congregation. You begin to think that they'll
never catch the vision or that they'll *never* grow up and stop acting like
children. We don't wake up one morning and find that we've become
cynical. It's like depression; it creeps up on us slowly. We don't even
know we've become more cynical until we catch ourselves saying
something negative about our parish or discover that our sense of humor
about our parishioners has a bite to it.

Disillusionment. Related to cynicism is a kind of disillusionment about
parish ministry in general or the church as a whole. We begin to wonder
whether if all churches were bombed tomorrow, our culture would miss
them. We begin to see the whole religious enterprise in our country
through dark-colored glasses. Then our whole call to ministry comes
into question.

Self-Depreciation. The literature on burnout talks about how victims of burnout tend to turn the sword inward. Like Bill Miller, they begin to blame themselves for what has gone sour in their ministry. They have a hard time seeing the contribution they have made to parish life. Rather than seeing burnout systemically, they view it only personally, and they don't feel very good about themselves.

So How Do I Avoid Burnout?

Burnout is a deeply religious issue because it forces us to confront how we perceive commitment to God and to the Kingdom. How can I call people to commitment Sunday after Sunday and not be committed myself? Doesn't the psalmist say, "The zeal of the Lord consumes me"? It takes fire to burn something up. It's one of the hazards of being consumed with a passion for God. The lukewarm folks don't make it. Mediocre people don't burn up like the zealots. Yet it's also the zealots who find themselves thrown out on the rubbish heap with the other dysfunctional leaders.

All great religious leaders eventually learn that they must do ministry within the confines of a human body. Having a body means being finite, having limits, being vulnerable to fatigue, illness, and death. All of us, to some degree or other, have run into the wall of human limitations. When we have pressed on beyond our limits it doesn't feel good at all, so we back off a bit while still holding on to goals important to us. This is called commitment.

The over-committed person, on the other hand, does not listen to the physical signs of being overextended. These people are so focused on their mission that they continually press on, ignoring the admonitions of friends and family and their body's increasing exhaustion. This is not commitment. In fact, we may need to question whether we are really serving idols or ego rather than the Kingdom. I do not believe God calls us to be physically and emotionally exhausted, cynical, disillusioned, and self-deprecating.

Burnout in the Bible

In his ministry on earth, Jesus never seemed to burn out. To this day I remain genuinely puzzled at how he did it. He knew he had to fulfill his mission within the confines of a human body. If I had had Jesus' deep compassion for the poor and the sick, and also his powers of healing, I would have healed people day and night without regard for my own health or rest. But Jesus didn't do that. The wondrous phrase that keeps showing up in the Gospels is "he dismissed the crowd." Then he went up into the mountains to pray, or to be alone with his disciples, or he got into a boat and went to sleep for awhile.

There's nothing particularly attractive about a burned-out preacher, but there was something powerfully attractive about Jesus. If he had burned out, the religious establishment of the day would not have found it necessary to kill him because burn-out victims are hardly a threat to politicians. As far as I can see, Jesus remained congruent with his message of offering new life to whoever came to hear or see him. I would call him a wholistic religious leader.

Other religious leaders in the Scriptures do show signs of burnout. Moses is a classic example. Moses was probably an Introvert who would have been quite content to herd sheep along a mountainside his entire life if the burning bush had not intervened. He was quite dazzling leading the children of Israel out of Egypt, but then he found himself in charge of a rather sizable community of wanderers. Soon his frustration, a sure sign of burnout, becomes apparent. He cries to God in anger and disgust, "Did I conceive all these people? Did I bring them forth that thou shouldst say to me, 'Carry them in your bosom, as a nurse carries the sucking child to the land which they didst swear to give their fathers'?" (Numbers 11:10). Moses wanted no part in playing nursemaid to a whining, stubborn group of malcontents. Later, he spent so much time up on the holy mountain with God that the people down below got tired and molded a golden calf. I wonder if Moses just couldn't bear to come back down and face the whining.

I contend that the first seminar on burnout was conducted on Mt. Sinai (Exodus 18:13-27). Moses' father-in-law, Jethro, watched this Introvert listening to people's problems from morning till evening. Listen to the wisdom of Jethro: "Moses," he says, "what you are doing is not good. You will destroy yourself and your people. Divide up this people into thousands, hundreds, fifties, and tens, and place able men over each group. And let them judge the people at all times. Every great matter they bring to you, but any small matter they shall decide themselves. So it will be easier for you, and they will bear the burden with you. If you do this, and God so commands you, then you will be able to endure, and all these people also will go to their place in peace." Wow! Sage advice for any leader. The way to endure is to delegate.

Yet near the end of his ministry, we find Moses going to God and saying, "God, if you are at all merciful, let me die right on the spot. Do not let me view my own misery any longer." That sounds like the exhausted cry of a burnout victim. I've been there. One becomes so miserable that death seems like a welcome rest.

Burnout is nothing to be ashamed of. Every effective leader has experienced it to some degree. Other characters in the Bible who manifest these characteristics are Saul, the first King of Israel, and possibly the prophet Jeremiah. If God is able to use people like this for the sake of the Kingdom, we are in good company.

Even the apostle Paul suffered from a period of burnout. In 2 Corinthians 1:8, Paul writes, "For we want to remind you, brothers, of the trouble we had in the province of Asia. The burdens laid upon us were so great and so heavy, that we gave up all hope of living. We felt that the sentence of death had been passed against us. But this happened so that we should rely, not upon ourselves, but only on God, who raises the dead. From such terrible dangers of death he saved us, and will save us; and we have placed our hope in him that he will save us again, as you help us by means of your prayers for us" (Good News). In this passage, Paul gives us a clear pathway out of burnout, namely, a deeper reliance uon God and a dependence on friends who earnestly hold us up in prayer. Indeed, support systems are a key ingredient in burn-out recovery. (We will explore this topic in Part Four.)

Reversing the Burnout Cycle: Expectations and Limitations

You can't fix a burned-out clergyperson the way you would a malfunctioning automobile, with a new set of spark plugs or a tune-up. Much more is required. First, we have to change our minds about ourselves. We have to accept our limitations, something that has never been easy for the human race. Although we would like to be as gods, coming to terms with our humanness is part of our spiritual journey here on earth. Second, we have to find the motivation to change. If we've reached the level of frustration in the burnout cycle, we're probably discontented and anxious enough to do something. If we've sunk down into apathy, it may take psychotherapy to cut through our denial enough so we can make a move one way or the other.

It's important to realize that you will probably find little encouragement from the church in confronting burnout. Our seminary training certainly doesn't teach us much about prevention. An Alban Institute study of newly ordained clergy who had been in a parish for at least three years confirmed that they had not been taught the basic survival skills –particularly stress management skills–needed to make an effective transition into a parish. Seasoned clergy claim that no one warned them about burnout and the ways it can destroy an otherwise good ministry.

These realities, plus the fact that one of five clergy may be suffering signs of burnout, lead me to believe that the church is grossly mismanaging its personnel. Further, religious communities aren't always merciful to the overcommitted. They take the best we've got, and when we run out of steam, they throw us out and replace us with someone else. That is not a cynical comment. We see the phenomenon all too often. Clergy firings continue to escalate. One study conducted by the Southern Baptist Sunday School Board in Nashville found that more than 2,100 Southern Baptist pastors had been fired during an eighteen-month period in 1989-90—an average of 116 a month and a thirty-one percent increase over 1984. Officials in the Georgia Baptist Convention estimate that one Southern Baptist minister loses his job every week. Burnout is often cited as a underlying cause of these firings.[2]

This is not meant to scare you, but to encourage you in your efforts at self-care. The ball is really in your court. There are resources to help you recognize the signs of burnout and reverse them before they ruin you. (This book is one of those resources.) But you'll have to take the initiative to avail yourself of them. Your health and ministry will depend on what you decide to do.

Cynics or Saints? The Redemptive Side of Burnout

For those of you who scored high on the Burnout Inventory, I want to add a redemptive note. The experience of burnout can be the passage way to a deeper reliance on the Grace of God, to a place of greater wholeness. The experience of burnout offers us the opportunity to wrestle with ministry priorities as they relate to our human limitations. Burnout can call us to a commitment to a healthier balance in ministry.

In an article in *Sojourners* magazine, Robert Sabath writes:

> Burnout is a refining fire that can detach us from an excessive identity with the results of our work and the impact we make in the world. It can teach us a deeper trust in God by forcing us to withdraw all hope, ideals, visions and expectations from every other object, situation, thing or person—except God....
>
> So burnout becomes not just stages of disillusionment, but if persisted in faithfully, it can become a maturing process of faith. Burnout de-establishes our illusions and establishes true faith. Both the cynic and the saint know the same discouraging realities of the world's pain and the difficulty by which any true healing and redemption come. The cynic withdraws and despairs of hope of any real change. The saint responds with faith, maintaining hope and zeal in the face of the many discouraging failures and partial embodiments of God's promise.
>
> Burnout holds the potential for making us either cynics or saints. In the midst of burnout, we have a choice. We can swing from the heights of all our unmet expectations to the detached withdrawal of no expectations at all. Or we can learn to grow in faith and transfer our misplaced expectations to the proper focus in God alone.[3]

Burnout thus can be the refiner's fire that moves us to a new level of awareness and trust in God.

CHAPTER 10

Rekindling the Fire: Al Tollefson's Story

When we last visited Al Tollefson in the introduction, he was trying hard to regain the vitality he had lost over the last two years. He knew he hadn't been giving Trinity much solid leadership. He was having a hard enough time simply taking care of the chronic dependents in the parish, plus attending all the meetings where he felt his presence was expected. Just back from vacation, he felt as exhausted as ever.

It was Thanksgiving when Al hit such a low point in fatigue and depression that he decided to see his conference minister. Al was beginning to question his call to ministry in general and particularly his call to Trinity. Al's conference minister listened to him for an hour, then made three suggestions: 1) Al should ask his consistory for an additional two weeks leave for rest and prayer; one of those weeks should be spent in silence at a monastery. 2) Al should locate a good therapist and begin to explore the dimensions of his depression. 3) Al should attend an Alban Institute seminar, "New Visions for the Long Pastorate," to further explore the issue of staying at Trinity or seeking another call.

It took Al two weeks to mull over the recommendations. He did not like the idea of letting the consistory know just how very fatigued he was. He knew he needed more rest, but there was enough of the remnant macho in him that he was afraid of looking like a crybaby. A couple of the consistory members were tough and driven, and they would tell him to buck up and get on with it. Seeking out a therapist was not to his liking either, but he felt he could keep that to himself and not tell the parish.

As it turned out, Al didn't ask for the two weeks extra leave, but he did ask the consistory to sponsor his attending the "New Visions for the Long Pastorate" seminar that spring. There he discovered that his burnout score was one of highest of twenty-eight participants. He learned more about burnout, about how it can leave you hollow, cynical, and disillusioned. He learned some key coping strategies to help him fight back, e.g., taking a periodic sabbatical (three months every four years). As to his staying at Trinity or leaving, he remained ambivalent. There were still some things he wanted to accomplish at Trinity, and the seminar helped him focus on those few goals.

After the seminar, Al began looking for a therapist in earnest. From his colleagues he got the names of several therapists to whom they referred parishioners. Al decided on Dr. John Simington, a psychiatrist, and by the third visit it was confirmed that Al was suffering from depression. The doctor recommended trying an antidepressant for a while. The drug did make him feel more energetic.

To his surprise, the consistory bought the idea of a sabbatical. After Al confided his malaise to two members on the consistory whom he trusted, they sold the idea for him. Three members were opposed to a sabbatical. After all, they felt, they worked hard too, and none of them got to go on sabbatical. But the rest of the consistory backed him. They believed in Al's competence and had seen him running out of gas over the past months. The final decision was to grant the sabbatical, but to couple it with some long-range planning and visioning, which was to take place before Al left.

The following summer, in addition to his vacation in July, Al went on sabbatical from August through the end of October. He spent some time at the Iona Spiritual Community in Scotland and the Taize Community in France. Then his wife Doris joined him for two weeks in the Holy Land. Back in the U.S. he spent several weeks as a pastor-in-residence at Princeton Theological Seminary in New Jersey. While there he spent most of his time in the library and attended chapel services when they were offered. The rest of the time he spent at home, repainting his house, listening to cassette tapes, and attending a different church in his area every Sunday. He did hear a few good sermons on his sabbatical, but the majority were mediocre to lousy. This did much to affirm his ability as a good preacher, and he began to look forward to getting back into harness. By November Al was a new person. His reading and reflecting had given him lots of new sermon ideas. He did not pick up the old job as he had left it. He had come to see that the parish was not using his best gifts by having him attend every committee that met at the church. He was going to delegate more and trust his lay leaders more. Besides, he needed to begin moving the parish toward the goals it had set just before he left on sabbatical. Al once again became the visionary leader who had brought the parish to life twelve years before.

In Search of New Heroes and Heroines

Al Tollefson survived his brush with burnout, and so can each of us. But first, we need to change our minds about what constitutes good pastoring and what constitutes good ministry in the world. In short, we need new heroes and heroines in the ordained ministry.

No longer can we hold up as models those hardy folks who manage to work seventy- to ninety-hour weeks and still survive. A lot of these "iron" types get elected as bishops and church executives after leading large congregations, and these are the ones who often press other clergy to follow their path. If we allow these people to be our heroes, we may all become sick or cynical.

Whatever our church role, we need to limit ourselves to fulfilling our ministry in fifty hours a week or less. Occasionally, we may need to work five or ten hours more than that per week, but that should be the exception. There is growing evidence that church professionals who consistently work longer than fifty hours per week usually suffer one or more of the following: 1) their bodies give out due to lack of rest, exercise, and good nutrition; 2) their relational lives suffer because of inadequate quality time with children, spouses, significant others; or 3) their spiritual lives suffer because there is little time to read, reflect, journal, pray, or get away for a retreat.

When one of these three areas suffers in our lives, not only are we the losers, but our congregations lose as well. When our bodies give out, the church has an invalid on its hands. We are more of a liability than an asset. When our relational life goes, we have little emotional energy to give to ministry. When our prayer life goes, our sermons and prayers lose depth.

In the next section we will take a more in-depth look at a number of self-care strategies that have helped church professionals overcome the effects of stress and burnout. As we have said several times already, the medium is the message when it comes to ministry. Self-care disciplines are not only for us, but for those we serve. We care for ourselves so that our congregations can have a whole, healthy person serving as their religious authority. We care for ourselves so that the message of faith, hope, and love can come through a glass clearly, not darkly.

PART FOUR

Self-Care Coping Strategies

CHAPTER 11

Living in the Tension

The difference between an effective and health-full ministry and a stressed-out, burned-out ministry can be described in one word: balance. Eliminating all stress from our lives is not the goal. Even if we could, we probably wouldn't like a stress-free life anyway. Avoiding all situations that might lead to burnout is not the goal either. To do that, we'd have to retreat to a mountaintop somewhere for the rest of our lives, and even then there would be no guarantees. What we're looking for is a way to be fully engaged in our ministries while maintaining our balance and our health. Self-care strategies will help us do just that, and we will explore a number of them in this section.

First, I want to take a closer look at the tension between self-care and ministry using a theory developed by a colleague at The Alban Institute, Barry Johnson, Ph.D. Barry believes that much of the stress of ministry comes from trying to resolve conflicts that cannot, and should not, be resolved. He calls these kinds of conflicts *polarities*. Polarities are like opposite sides of a coin. No matter how hard we try, we can't make the two sides become one side. Unlike our traditional understanding of conflicts, polarities can never be resolved; they can only be managed, more or less well.[1]

Here's how a polarity works: One set of parishioners complains that their clergy person is too rigid, doesn't listen, and is a dictator of sorts. Another congregation complains that their pastor is too ambiguous and wishy-washy.

These two types of complaints might be pictured this way.

```
        +                           +


                        D │ B
                        A │ C
        rigidity              ambiguity


        ─                           ─
```

Rigidity and ambiguity are identified above as negative aspects of a polarity. Missing in the upper quadrants of this chart are the positive aspects of the polarity. Not surprisingly, one can fill the quadrants by listening to parishioners talk about what they like in their minister. For example, the "rigid" pastor often gets this type of praise: "She is always clear. You always know where she stands." The "ambiguous" pastor is often told, "You're flexible. You always listen to reason." With this input we can create a more complete picture.

```
    +                                   +

            clear               flexible
                        D │ B
                        A │ C
            rigid               ambiguous


    ─                                   ─
```

This model is based on the assumption that every polarity has positive aspects (+) and negative aspects (-). To manage polarities well, we need to see both sides as part of the complete picture.

The Gestalt concept of figure/ground is useful in understanding polarities.

The picture to the right is a classic. Is it a goblet or two heads facing each other? The answer is, "It depends on how you look at it." When the goblet is most prominent (figure) the heads become a part of the background (ground). When the heads become figure, the goblet becomes ground.

So if someone says, "This is a picture of a goblet," she is accurate. When another says, "It's two heads," he also is accurate. What is figure for one is ground for the other. Both are accurate, but neither is complete.

Church congregations are very much like that goblet/two heads picture. Our first impression is like a snapshot; we see the system frozen in place. Even after several years we still may not have experienced the total cycle of the organism. We need to see how the system regulates itself and responds to both internal and external pressure. Over time we begin to sense how all the parts fit together as a functional whole.

One of the most important polarities pastors must deal with is self-care/ministry to others. How do we maintain some kind of balance between our service to others and our care for ourselves and our own needs? Let's look at this dilemma through the lens of polarity theory.

What are all the things that would draw us into greater self care?	What are all the things that draw us deeply into a ministry to and with others?
Self Care Ⓒ Ⓐ	**Ministry to Others**
What are some of the negative consequences of being Ⓓ drawn too deeply into self care? The cost of over-indulging in self care.	Ⓑ What are some of the negative consequences of being drawn too deeply into ministry to others? The cost of over-extending.

Below is a composite of clergy responses about the polarities in their ministry. When I do the polarities exercise in workshops, I am always amazed to see how quickly the group can completely fill in the four quadrants of the chart. As you can see, getting stuck in quadrant D is as negative as being stuck in quadrant B. The negative side of Self-Care can be as bad as the down side of Ministry to Others.

Quadrant C	Quadrant A
+	+
Health and personal vitality	Meaning and purpose in life
Greater longevity	Loving and caring for others
Valuing self	Connectedness with others
Being pro-active towards self	Dialogue and learning
Allowing others to care for you	Offering self for the sake
	of a broken world.
SELF-CARE	**MINISTRY TO OTHERS**
Quadrant D	Quadrant B
−	−
Self-Indulgence	Loss of self
Narcissism	Burnout
Being isolated and unconnected	Feeling exploited and abused
Idolatry of the body and health	Cynicism, disillusionment,
Getting locked into rituals that	self-depreciation
are self-serving	Thoughts of suicide
Addictions	

True to the theory of polarities, the way out of the down side of one polarity is to become attracted to the positive side of the opposite pole. How do we pull ourselves out of cynicism and overwork in the ministry? By beginning to take care of ourselves. If we're stuck in self-indulgence and narcissism, how do we get out of it? By finding someone in worse shape than we are and doing something for them. It is our ability to care deeply for someone else and act on that caring that draws us out of the snake hole of self-absorption. Suddenly our life takes on a whole new meaning. We have a purpose for living again.

But watch the polarity. If a little bit of helping someone else feels good, then why not help a whole lot of people all the time? Because before you know it, you'll be headed for the negative side of other care, i.e., burnout. Johnson calls this the One Pole Myth. He claims that the longer we stay on one pole, the more likely we are to sink into the negative side of that pole. The trick is to live most of our lives in the positive quadrants of both of the two poles.

Of course, remaining totally in the positive sections of the two poles all the time is impossible. Often it is the very sensation of sinking into the negative side of one pole that propels us into the positive side of the other. But wouldn't it be nice to find that perfect spot on the boundary between the two positive quadrants and just stand there? Yes, but according to Johnson, that won't work either. He calls this the Merged Poles Myth. Life is never so static that we could stand between the poles for long. The balance that worked yesterday may not work today. The world around us changes; our bodies are constantly changing; everything is in flux. It's like the balancing beam a tightrope walker carries. That beam is rarely held steady. It moves up and down to keep the walker balanced on the high wire.

In reality, we will always be oscillating between the two poles. In the best of all worlds, our oscillating will be mostly between the positive quadrants of the poles, but there will be times when we sink into the negative quadrants. What we want to avoid is a kind of wild oscillating from the negative of one pole to the positive of the other that comes as a result of a crisis, for example, you're totally burned out and your spouse tells you she's leaving unless you do something right now. Over time, we want to become aware enough of ourselves that we can make the move out of the negative quadrants at the first sign of trouble. Our life path would then look something like the following:

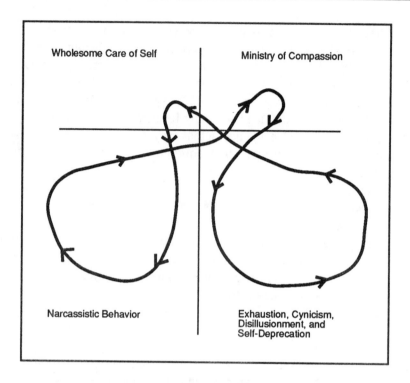

I find it tragic that many of the clergy I meet in workshops are spending the majority of their lives in the down side of both poles.

Having been caught in the self-indulgence cycle before, I know how hard it is to move to Quadrant C in a meaningful way. How much easier it is to down a couple of beers, order a large pepperoni pizza with extra cheese, and plop down in front of the TV. Getting out of the deadly cycle between burnout and narcissistic self-serving behavior requires taking baby steps, like going for a walk instead of having that extra piece of cake. That gets me feeling a little better about myself. Then I may call a friend and together we might find time to wedge in a luncheon date. My friend then fortifies me even more in doing good things for myself. With that light at the end of the tunnel, I am able to take the steps needed to get my diet back under control and my exercise regimen back on track.

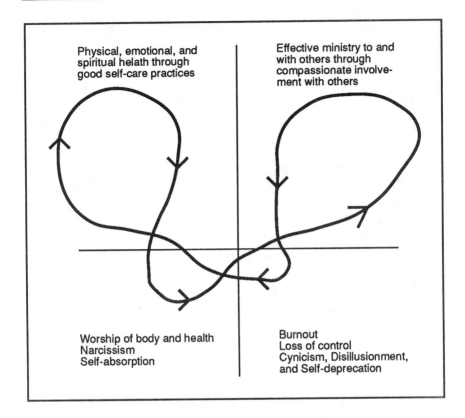

Physical, emotional, and spiritual helath through good self-care practices

Effective ministry to and with others through compassionate involvement with others

Worship of body and health
Narcissism
Self-absorption

Burnout
Loss of control
Cynicism, Disillusionment, and Self-deprecation

As the polarities model reminds us, we clergy are called by God not only to the positive side of the ministry pole but to the positive side of the self-care pole as well. We are called, first and foremost, to become whole ourselves, and second, to help others catch the vision of this wholeness. The one is as important as the other.

In the next few chapters, we'll take a look at some specific self-care strategies that can help us keep that balance in our ministries and in our lives. The practices you adopt to achieve and maintain your health will not be the same as the ones I use. We must each find the combination of strategies that fits us—our temperaments, our metabolisms, our lifestyles.

Some of the strategies will be aimed specifically at countering the effects of stress; others will target the symptoms of burnout. Some will address both the twin destroyers—stress and burnout. Review each of them briefly, noting those that might work for you and your situation.

Be aware that several of the strategies may require more time than others. To give those strategies your best shot, you may want to try them during a low-activity period during the year. From my experience, the best time to take on a new personal discipline is when we are not feeling overwhelming stress.

These coping strategies are designed as alternatives to the many destructive ways of coping with stress or burnout, such as drugs, alcohol, pornography, spouse and child abuse, unconscious eating, television binges, promiscuity, buying sprees, anorexia, and bulimia. The more disciplines we can take on, the less we will need our current dependencies.

I encourage you to approach these strategies with a sense of light-heartedness and grace. Experiment with those that appeal to you. Get hooked on one or two, if that seems helpful. But recognize that it is the process of learning to take care of ourselves that is the ultimate goal, not mastering new activities. After all, self-care should help reduce our stress not increase it!

Let's begin!

". . . and this is where our pastor lives."

CHAPTER 12

The Spiritual Uplift

Jesus Savior pilot me,
Over life's tempestuous sea.
Unknown waves before me roll,
Hiding rock and treacherous shoal
Chart and compass come from Thee,
Jesus Savior pilot me.

This old hymn certainly speaks to the dilemma of stress in modern times.
When flux, change, and transition make us sick unto death, the bedrock
of spiritual practices can serve as a sure support—reading the Psalms,
singing old familiar hymns, receiving holy communion, being cared for
by the people our churches bring together.

We expect our religious communities to help us as we go through
life's transitions: birth, death, marriage, rites of passage into adulthood,
etc. The church does a good job with some transitions, e.g., marriage,
confirmation, and not so well with others. e..g., divorce, retirement, a
move to a nursing home. As pastors, we may not always find spiritual
nuture in our churches, so rediscovering some spiritual practices that
help us deal with stress and burnout may take us beyond the organized
church.

It's a well-recognized fact that a deep spiritual life can counter the
effects of stress. V. Frankl, in his book *From Death Camp to Existential-
ism,* wanted to know why some of those living in the death camps died
before reaching the ovens while others managed to survive. He says that
the survivors had a "will to meaning." No matter how bad things got,
they never gave up hope. They would not accept the judgment of their

captors. They believed that the God who delivered his people from en-
slavement in Egypt would somehow deliver them as well. In short, it
was their faith that kept them alive.

This is an extreme example of how spiritual depth can neutralize the
bad chemistry of stress. People of faith tend to be better anchored than
others in times of stress and transition. They bring a kind of perspective
to life, knowing that death is only the beginning of new life, a transition
from this world to the next.

Spiritual depth also seems to be an antidote to burnout. Many of the
spiritual giants of the past acknowledge that pain and adversity were
their greatest teachers. They did not go out to find the "hair shirt," but
when it was handed to them they wore it. Though they had times of
physical and emotional fatigue, cynicism, disillusionment, and self-
depreciation (signs of burnout), they eventually found a way to rise up in
peace and gratitude. What made these spiritual giants different from
others is that they refused to take the easy way out through self-pity or
denial.

Anything we do to enrich our spiritual lives will help us turn our
adversity into a refiner's fire. Burnout tends to come when our self-
perceptions get distorted by ego or erroneous beliefs about reality. But if
we can look reality in the face, adversity can be a spiritual gift. Indeed,
the truth shall make us free.

Unfortunately, the majority of us clergy were sent to our places of
ministry with a minimal amount of support or training in spiritual formation. Somehow, between courses in theology and the Bible, plus daily
chapel attendance, we budding pastors were supposed to develop into
spiritual giants. Yet, in the three years I spent in a Lutheran seminary,
not once did anyone ask me if I prayed, if I had any difficulties in my
prayer life, or whether I practiced any sort of "rule of life." They may
have asked me about my Christology, but not if I believed in Christ.

After seminary, I imagined that things would be different when I
was an ordained pastor in my own congregation. After all, I would
regularly be dealing with the Word and sacrament, prayer and worship.
Surely my spiritual life would improve. Unfortunately, it didn't. I
expected people to come to me with deep theological questions about
their faith. But the only theological discussion I can recall took place in
an adult education class. A parishioner wanted to know the difference
between the immortality of the soul and the resurrection of the body.

Being academically trained in theology, I blasted him out of the water with a heady answer. He never came back to the class. Looking back, I'm glad no one came to me with a problem in their prayer life. I probably would have had little to offer beyond what I had learned in confirmation class. Over time, parish ministry drained me spiritually, rather than uplifting me. I had not been taught any pathways out of the desert of spiritual emptiness, even though I was seen by my parishioners as the expert on spirituality.

Among my clergy friends there often seemed to be a conspiracy of silence when it came to our spiritual lives. There were times when I would have liked to ask, "Hey, what do the rest of you do when you try to pray and it's like sawdust in your mouth?" What kept me from asking was the impression I got from other clergy that they had few problems, least of all a spiritual problem. How easily I bought into the practice of pretending I had it all together too!

Pastors face unique problems, I believe, in keeping fresh spiritually. For one thing, the spiritual disciplines we learned as children and young adults are now the tools of our trade. For me, scripture, prayer, and worship became overfamiliar and lost much of their mystery. It was difficult to read the Bible devotionally when I knew I had to prepare a sermon from those texts. I felt so much pressure to come up with something meaningful to say that I read the Bible as though I were on a scavenger hunt! Everything I read was directed toward others' spiritual needs and not my own. I was doing so much praying with other people in hospitals, in homes, and prior to meetings that I stopped praying on my own. I failed to recognize the essential difference between nurturing the spiritual journey of another and having a unique spiritual journey of my own.

The Dilemma of Parish Ministry

The following diagram helps describe the dilemma clergy face in nurturing their spiritual lives:

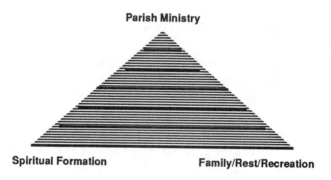

    Parish Ministry

Spiritual Formation   Family/Rest/Recreation

To have a vibrant parish ministry, we need the strong base provided by good primary relationships, spiritual nurture, and adequate rest. Unfortunately, parish ministry is so demanding that it can easily preempt the other aspects of our lives. Most married clergy have experienced tension between family responsibilities and parish demands. Single clergy may not experience as many demands from significant people in their lives, but they are just as vulnerable to the consuming nature of parish ministry. Some clergy manage these tensions well. I did not. I continually over-functioned in the parish and consequently under-functioned in my marriage.

When we realize that we and our families both need time away from the parish, a collision occurs on the right side of the triangle.

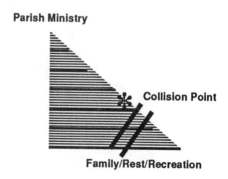

Parish Ministry

Collision Point

Family/Rest/Recreation

A collision point can also occur on the other side of the triangle, between parish ministry and our spiritual formation.

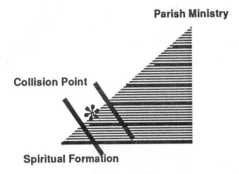

Parish Ministry

Collision Point

Spiritual Formation

I continually find that clergy have a very difficult time managing this tension point. Many clergy feel guilty for taking time for their own personal spiritual feeding; they regard it as selfish. They do not realize that, unless regular time is taken, they will not have the spiritual depth to sustain a healthy ministry.

The way to keep a congregation vital is to be a vital, growing person in their midst. Clergy don't need more knowledge or skills as much as they need a deeper spiritual life. Protecting time for spiritual nurture will be much easier if you have a cadre of lay people who understand the connection between their parish's spiritual life and the spiritual life of their pastor. These lay leaders will be able to go to bat for you when you need a sabbatical, continuing education, or time away at a monastery for reflection, journaling, and prayer. They will understand that you must have time in your daily schedule for practicing a spiritual discipline. And they will be aware that when their pastor is alive, healthy, and growing, they will be nurtured spiritually as well.

For some clergy a collision point occurs between their personal relational life and their spiritual formation, but this is less common.

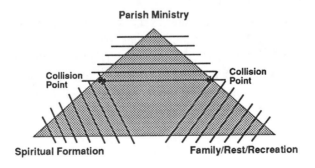

Parish Ministry

Collision Point   **Collision Point**

Spiritual Formation   **Family/Rest/Recreation**

A clergyman with a young family confided that he would get little resistance from his congregation if he said he wanted to spend three nights a year at a local monastery to reflect and pray. But his spouse and children would not be as understanding. They barely tolerated the evenings and weekends he spent at the church and would take it personally if he said he needed time alone for spiritual renewal.

Discovering Spiritual Disciplines

Spiritual disciplines can be for us the regular pathways by which we open ourselves to the Grace of God. They can become the process by which we allow our own emptiness, our lack of perspective, our self-image—yes, even our hubris—to be confronted with the Holy. Spiritual disciplines can help restore us to a sense of being whole, forgiven, and at peace.

Of course, no discipline is ever sure-fire. We may not experience something we would identify as Grace every time. We are always vulnerable and dependent, and whatever discipline we choose, we are bound to encounter desert times. At those times, we may need help to get unstuck. When my private prayer life stopped feeding me as a newly ordained pastor, I simply stopped praying. With some help I might have been able to rediscover the living stream, but once I lost the discipline, I also stopped putting myself in a place where I could find some connection with God. That was disastrous.

With any spiritual discipline, there is always the danger that it can become an end in itself. For example, the Scribes and Pharisees in the New Testament observed all the outward disciplines of fasting, temple rituals, and Sabbath observance, but did not experience the deeper spiritual essence of these practices.

Many of the clergy I encounter in seminars and workshops these days are turning to other disciplines besides the traditional scripture, prayer, and worship to stay alive spiritually. The following are some of the spiritual disciplines that appear to nurture the clergy I meet. True to our understanding of wholistic health, each of these disciplines also promotes emotional and physical well-being.

Meditation

Meditation has often been thought of as a religious activity, particularly in connection with eastern religions, especially Buddhism. Today, stress centers across the country are teaching people how to meditate to deal with the tension in their lives. But the discipline of meditation is more than a secular stress-reduction technique or a form of Eastern piety. We need to reclaim this spiritual discipline from our own early Christian heritage.

First, let's acknowledge that meditation does promote health. It allows us to quiet our minds and relax our bodies so that the fight-or-flight stress response is not triggered. Dr. Herbert Benson, author of *The Relaxation Response*[1], has documented its medical effects in his research on the practice of Transcendental Meditation.

Blood Pressure and Pulse

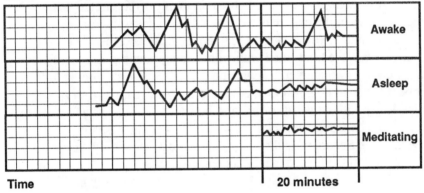

Because of these proven medical outcomes, stress centers, often connected with local hospitals, have adopted meditation as a treatment method. Usually patients are advised to count their breaths up to four and then repeat the process over and over again. When patients' minds begin to wander, they are instructed simply to let those thoughts pass by like clouds in the sky and return to the gentle counting of breaths. It sounds simple, but it rarely is. The more stressed the person is, the more difficult it is to focus on the counting of the breath rather than all the things that have gone haywire in his or her life. Our minds are constantly on the lookout, preparing us for any eventuality. We scan the future to see if anything should concern us. Inevitably, we find something and, when we do, the fight/flight stress reaction pumps a little adrenaline into our systems. Our minds also survey past events, evaluating them to see if anything has happened about which we should be concerned. Eventually, we find something like, "Oh, I wish I hadn't said that in front of my boss yesterday." And the same reaction occurs. But when we manage to keep our minds completely in the present moment, there is nothing about which we need to be concerned. There is simply God, us, and this moment in time.

It is at this point that meditation becomes something more than a relaxation technique. The early Christian mystics called meditation "contemplative prayer" and practiced it often. Gerald May, in his book *Will and Spirit*[2], describes contemplation as an uncluttered appreciation of existence, a state of mind or condition of the soul that is simultaneously wide-awake and free from all preoccupation, preconception, and interpretation. The mystics felt it was impossible to contain God in words or images, so they simply tried, in their prayer time, to be open and receptive to the experience of God.

In seminary, you may have learned the difference between kataphatic prayer, the kind filled with words, images, and concepts of God that we use in worship, and apophatic prayer, which is listening to God or being open to however God comes to us. Apophatic prayer is not completely without words or images, however. Using a sacred word or phrase can help keep our focus on God. The early Christians of the Alexandrian School used the Jesus prayer most frequently: "Lord Jesus Christ, Son of God, have mercy upon me a sinner," or the short form, "Lord have mercy." The Greek phrase "kyrie eleison" was probably the Christian mantra used by eastern Christians. The book *The Way of a Pilgrim*[3] details how this form of contemplative prayer was introduced into western Christianity by a wandering Russian monk.

When an individual is doing manual labor, such as seeding a grain field, it is possible to have a phrase like this going on in one's mind throughout the whole day. Biblical scholars attribute this form of prayer to St. Paul's admonishment to "pray without ceasing." (1 Thess. 5:17) There are times when I'm running, walking, or swimming when the cadence of my bodily movement allows certain phrases to become repetitive in my mind. When I become conscious that the phrase that is stuck in my mind's grooves is not particularly helpful to me, I consciously choose another phrase to replace it. Some of the phrases I use when I consciously sit and meditate include:

I am, Thou art
Kyrie Eleison
I am the Beloved of God
Holy
Yahweh, Yeshua, Ruach   *(Hebrew for God, Jesus, Spirit)*
O Great Spirit
Come Lord Jesus

The quality of my day is different when I take fifteen minutes before I rush out the door to move into this meditative space. In fact, it is so different that I am always mystified that I don't do more of it. I try to keep the practice going throughout the day by attaching it to a certain trigger, e.g., sitting at a red light or in an airplane ready to take off. If you would like to experiment with this form of prayer, I recommend that you:

1) Find a way you can be seated with your chest, neck, and head in a straight line (on pillows against a wall or in a firm straight-back chair).

2) Determine precisely how long you intend to meditate and stay with that commitment regardless of what transpires. To begin with, I would suggest periods no longer than fifteen or twenty minutes.

3) Choose a sacred word or phrase and wrap your intention to focus this time on God in that word or phrase. Begin repeating it in time with your breath.

4) Be gentle with yourself. Everyone needs to struggle to keep his or her mind focused in this way. When your mind becomes flooded with outside thoughts, experiment with labeling what your mind is bringing to your attention, i.e., planning, critiquing, brainstorming, the distraction of noise or physical discomfort, lusting, projecting, etc. It's a way of letting each thought go through you without getting hooked on any one of them.

5) Try to become passive to your environment; for example, if noise is distracting you, rather than trying to push it away, simply accept it as a given for the moment. It may be a manifestation of God that you have failed to recognize or an aspect of God's creation that you have missed. Try to find something redemptive in the distraction so you don't put energy into trying to repress it.

6) Try to keep your body as still as possible. A restless body is a sign of a restless mind. When your body keeps shifting to become more comfortable, it has a way of controlling your mind.

7) Get into the observer mode if you can. It is possible to be in a mode of consciousness in which you watch, with some detachment, your body, your feelings, your thoughts, none of which detract from your simply being "the watcher."

8) Keep a journal of your experience during the meditative time. This can be a brief reflective time in which you note feelings, discomforts, thoughts of where God was manifest during that time, etc. There may be more happening than you thought while in the meditative state.

9) When you get stuck (many do and quit), find a teacher to get you through the desert spots.

10) Try gazing at a lit candle or a religious symbol. For some people, closed eyes are more distracting than helpful.[4]

This practice is normally easier for Introverts than Extraverts, although Extraverts at certain points in their lives often have a real desire to develop their interior processes.

Meditation can be a potent growth vehicle for all of us but especially for men. Our culture still programs men to be out of touch with their feelings and their bodies. The message is: "If you are a real man, you will ignore physical pain and soft feelings." It is a tragedy that we live alienated from our bodies and feelings because during times of illness we tend to ignore what our bodies are telling us. The physical symptoms may be blaring loud and clear that a man is about to have a heart attack, yet he will usually plow ahead unaware of the danger. The practice of meditation can be an awakening for such men. They will notice bodily sensations as well as feelings, all emanating from the center of consciousness called the "observer."

Journaling

Some people find working with their thoughts and feelings through the written word to be their most profound spiritual discipline. There are a number of ways to go about keeping a journal. One of the most popular, and perhaps most profound, is the Intensive Journal developed by Ira Progoff, a student of Carl Jung. Three-day Progoff seminars guiding people in keeping an Intensive Journal are offered all over North America.

Progoff makes a distinction between keeping a diary and working with a journal. A journal involves much more than recording the events of your life. When used effectively, keeping a journal can be as profound an intervention in your life as psychotherapy or spiritual direction. When the process works well, we discover something new about ourselves each time we do an exercise. The process of writing in this way can bring about a breakthrough in personal and spiritual awareness.

The Intensive Journal idea begins with the premise that we live on a variety of levels. We go about our lives trying to cope on a day-to-day basis, yet underneath we struggle with deeper issues and other levels of self-awareness. Each time we have a dialogue with our various "selves," we are able to unearth some of these issues.

About a dozen different sections in Progoff's Intensive Journal allow journal keepers to work on various levels. For example, in a section called the "period log" we are to describe briefly four to eight periods in our lives up to the present. We note issues we struggled with in each period and the event that marked the beginning of that period. The "period log" can be rewritten from time to time as we review our history in the light of current issues and struggles.

In the "daily log," we reflect on how we feel upon awakening in the morning. We describe moods and sensations and record such things as the thoughts that kept coming into our minds unbidden. We identify worries, hopes, fantasies, and emotions, and at the end of the day we record how the whole day felt.

The "dialogue with persons" invites us to write out a dialogue with persons with whom we are in relationship—perhaps persons whose impact on us remains unclear. (They may be living or dead, peers or parents or parent figures.)

Because we grow inside while we are engaged with activity on the outside, the section "dialogue with works" invites us to write out the meaning of our current work or our past work. Works have their own value, their own requirements. They shape us in particular ways, and we tend to define ourselves by them. Hence, having a dialogue with our work gives us rich opportunities to understand what our work symbolizes for us.

These descriptions should give you some idea of the rich opportuni-

ties for insight available in the Progoff Journal. I encourage you to
attend a Progoff workshop if you can. I found the workshop to be a
wonderful time to pull together the ragged edges of my life. If you can't
attend a workshop, get a copy of Progoff's book *At a Journal Workshop*.[5]

Keeping a journal of this kind isn't for everyone, but for some of
you this discipline will open many doors to your inner life.

Spiritual Director/Spiritual Friend

If I were to choose one discipline to undergird all the others, it would be
meeting regularly with a spiritual director. When I was in seminary, no
one mentioned anything about spiritual directors or friends. Today, more
seminary graduates know something about spiritual direction, and some
have actually been in direction.

To determine whether a spiritual director would be of help to you,
ask yourself, "Who is my pastor?" Most of us believe in pastoring
others, but don't see that need for ourselves. Some of you may think
your bishop or judicatory executive is your pastor, and these church
leaders no doubt would like to be that for you. But if they're honest,
they will tell you that, given their dual roles of administrator and over-
seer of church structures, there's just no time for this type of ministry. A
few middle judicatories actually call someone specifically to be a pastor
to clergy and their families. As long as he or she has no other heavy
responsibilities in the judicatory, this person might be a spiritual director
for you. However, you would want to make sure that he or she has some
training in spiritual guidance, and then develop a specific contract about
your relationship.

The majority of clergy I work with have no one who relates to them
in this special way, no one who pays particular attention to them and
their spiritual journey and with whom they regularly structure time to
review their spiritual path.

For the past eight years I have been in direction with an Irish
Catholic laywoman who works with the Shalem Institute for Spiritual
Formation in Washington, D.C. She has saved my hide more that a few
times. On two separate occasions, she urged me to get psychotherapeutic
help, while remaining clear that spiritual direction was not therapy. At
some of my lowest points she effectively helped me see how special I am
in the eyes of God and how deeply God cares for me. Because of her

humor and caring, I continue to look forward to our monthly time to-gether. I pay her $55 per session, and it's one of the best investments I make in my well-being.

I have found spiritual direction particularly helpful when I hit a dry spot in practicing spiritual disciplines. When we take on any type of spiritual discipline, inevitably—*I repeat, inevitably*—we will run into a brick wall along the way to deeper spiritual awareness. Every one of us clergy at some point has resolved to pray and read the Bible daily. What happened to that commitment? Usually, we hit some kind of desert spot, get discouraged, and quit. Then we lay a guilt trip on ourselves because we feel less disciplined and spiritual than others.

A spiritual director can be very useful when we hit these barriers. Usually a spiritual director has experienced the same desert spots in her or his spiritual journey and can help you find a way back to the oasis that discipline offered you earlier.

Some people I've talked to are a little suspicious of spiritual direc-tion. They wonder what happened to the doctrine of the priesthood of all believers. We are all equal at the foot of the cross, right? Why do we need an intermediary to be our priest before God? We can go directly to God ourselves. While it's true that we are all justified by Grace through our faith, we are not all at the same level in our growth in Grace. The process of sanctification is at work in us until the day we die. So there is always something more we can learn from a spiritual mother or father. This growth does not add one iota to our standing as redeemed children of God, but it does help us move more deeply into joy, gratitude, and amazement at the bounty of God. And our spiritual growth helps us greatly in being spiritual mentors to our parishioners.

Your spiritual journey is different from that of any other person alive. Spiritual direction helps you see what is special about your spiri-tual struggles. If we can understand how our perception of reality differs from others', we are in a much better place to nurture ourselves spiritu-ally. What works for your parishioners may not work well for you.

Finding a Spiritual Director

The first thing you look for in a spiritual director is, of course, a depth of spirituality that you feel might be helpful to you. We need to know that this person likes and cares about us, and we need to like and respect the person in return. We may have to investigate and "test out" suitable persons before we make a commitment to the process. I believe we Protestant clergy do well to look within the Catholic tradition for persons with calling and skill in this vocation. The Roman Catholic church has a much longer tradition in spiritual direction than the Protestant church. There are some exceptions, however. Groups like the Shalem Institute for Spiritual Formation offer intensive training to persons called to this ministry. A demanding two-year training program helps persons of various faith traditions deepen their ministries as spiritual guides.[6] Other persons offering training are Roy Fairchild at San Francisco Theological Seminary in San Anselmo, California; and Jack Biersdorf at the Ecumenical Theological Center in Detroit, Michigan.[7]

It may be difficult for some of you to find a person who has been trained in spiritual direction. But most of you know someone whose spirituality you respect and with whom you could meet on a regular basis for mutual support in your spiritual quests. This kind of person is usually referred to as a spiritual friend. The relationship is slightly different from that with a spiritual director, but it remains a discipline. The two of you agree to pray for one another and to meet periodically to deal with aspects of your spiritual lives that don't seem to be working well. You help each other out of the stuck spots. For help in developing this kind of relationship, I recommend *Spiritual Friend,* by my colleague Tilden Edwards.[8]

Chanting

In chanting, as in meditation, you take a basic biblical or theological theme and work with it for a time. Usually the themes are somewhat longer than the word or phrase used in meditation. It is the theme's simplicity and repetitiveness that give it its power.

I discovered the powerful benefits of chanting quite by accident. Stress management had taught me to limit the amount of information I took in each day, so I began turning off my car radio while driving. By having the radio on all the time, I believe I was teaching myself *not* to listen. After all, when you have words coming at you all the time, you have to tune some of them out or you become overwhelmed. Yet as a pastor I needed to keep my listening skills well-honed. I decided that my car radio was working against me.

So, one Monday morning when I was trying to reach the airport on time, I began singing a simple refrain I had learned in a meditation class. I continued to sing through two huge traffic snarls, and when I actually *missed* the plane, which in my business is really bad news, I wasn't too upset about it. The chant had taken me to a place of unusual calm. Now, whenever I'm in the car, I chant. It takes me slightly over an hour to reach an airport or my office in the city, so forty-five minutes of the drive can be spent singing one chant. The chant I choose depends on my disposition and what kind of spiritual nurture I seem to need at the time.

I often teach chants in seminars, and inevitably I get calls a few weeks later requesting that I sing one or the other over the phone. As a defense against this, I have developed an audio-cassette tape of some of my favorite chants used while driving my car; I call them "Chants For the Road."[10] In the years since discovering this spiritual discipline, I've also been collecting chant tapes from all over the country. Life Structure Resources markets six to eight of the best ones I know.[11]

Christians in North America have yet to catch on to the power of chanting. According to Neurolinguistic Programming theory, chanting is powerful because we are anchoring the words of a chant into our consciousness with a combination of sound, feelings, and images. Emile Durkheim claims you can win people's loyalty for life if you give them a meaningful experience and then bind that experience to a ritual or song. Anytime you sing that song, people will recall the experience.

In the early church, liturgical rituals reminded people of their conversion to the faith. These days, our rituals may seem empty because we have failed to give people the powerfully meaningful experience that merges with the song or ritual.

Two communities that use chanting to great effect are the Taize community in France and the Sidda Yoga community in South Ballston, New York and Garnishpuri, India.

The Taize community centers much of its worship on lengthy chants. Because people come from all over the world to experience the spirituality of Taize, many of their chants are in Latin. To experience the Taize chants, I recommend the cassette tape "Taize Cantate" by Jacques Berthier.[11]

One United Church of Christ minister related his experience of using a chant in worship. He took one of the simple three-line chants I had taught at a workshop and asked his choir to sing it during the distribution of communion. The choir was insulted that he would give them something so simple and mundane to sing, but the pastor convinced them to give it a try. After the service, the chant was all the people could talk about. It made a deep impact on the people precisely because of its simplicity. The repetition of the words combined with music embeds a simple biblical or theological concept in the psyche.

Most of us like to sing things we know. The advantage of a chant is that it becomes familiar very quickly. I believe the things that are committed to memory easily have the greatest impact on us. When people are on their deathbed, what is it they usually want? Something familiar that has been committed to memory—the Twenty-third Psalm, the Lord's Prayer, a favorite hymn. Chanting helps people commit to memory some of the rich religious themes that can transform their lives.

For busy people, chanting while driving alone can be an important spiritual discipline. If you can't seem to find the time to pray, singing a single chant over a period of time may work for you. It's a good way to redeem the down time while driving. I used the first chant I learned for two years before learning another one. Since then I have been collecting chants, using different ones for different purposes. If you want to begin immediately, take one verse of your favorite hymn and stay with it for twenty to thirty minutes. A hymn verse I often use is:

Breathe on me breath of God
Fill me with life anew
That I may love what thou doest love
And do what thou wouldst do.

That chant will take you one hundred miles with more still to learn from it. Here are a few other chants I like:

1) The first chant is based on the Scripture passage "I am the vine, you are the branches. Except you abide in me you do not have life."

Thy care and calm, deep mystery
Evermore deeply, rooted in thee

2) Here's a chant I use whenever I'm feeling particularly down and discouraged:

Gentle, loving God, the Mother of my soul
Hold me as your own

3) Here's a chant developed by Gerald G. May, Director of Training at the Shalem Institute for Spiritual Formation:

God call us home.
Christ make us one.
Holy Spiritu come.
Love will be done.

4) A favorite chant of mine from the Taize community:

Adoramus Te Domini

(roughly translated, "You who have dominion over us, we adore you.")

Fasting

A Korean Presbyterian pastor taught me the power of fasting many years ago. At one of my transition seminars, he confided that he would never have endured some of the pressures in his parish had it not been for the discipline of fasting. He fasted regularly for four or five days at a time. He was shocked at how little was known about fasting and how little it was practiced in this country. Since that time I have committed myself to at least two five-day fasts each year. I most enjoy conducting the Holy Week fasts at the Shalem Institute in Washington, D.C.

There are three important reasons I recommend this spiritual discipline:

1. It aligns us with the one third of the world that goes to bed hungry every day. When one part of the body is in pain, we all hurt. Fasting can put us in touch with that corporate pain.

2. Fasting is one of the healthier things you can do for your body. Scientific research indicates that whenever we stop consuming solid food, our body engages in a process called autolysis whereupon it feeds upon itself for energy. During this process, the body in its wisdom feeds upon the worst parts of the self and eliminates them from the system—

damaged cells, sick cells, fatty tissue with toxic chemicals stored in them. One research study discovered that people who were fasting had ten times the amount of toxins in their urine as those on a regular diet. Fasting should thus be seen as a cleansing process. The body uses those times for rubbish disposal.

This is one of the reasons why a shorter fast can be more difficult than a longer fast done less frequently. Generally, the first day of a fast I am slightly ill and need to go to bed early. I've since learned that the body dumps its largest load of toxins into the system during the first twenty-four hours of a fast. The second day of a fast, I usually find my energy starting to build. I do some of my most creative writing while fasting.

3. As a spiritual discipline, fasting has proven to be a time of purification and deep prayer for the saints of old. Every major religion has had fasting as part of its tradition. Scripture often refers to fasting in combination with prayer. It's as though the fasting adds something unique to one's prayer life. The mind seems to remain much clearer when fasting, hence the ability to be much more focused in prayer.

Even considering the discipline of fasting may be difficult for some of you because as a spiritual practice it is alien to our culture. We live in an era in which overconsumption of food has become an epidemic problem. Our refrigerators and deep freezes are always fully stocked, and our microwave ovens are so handy we can make whatever we want in a few minutes. A high percentage of North Americans have little discipline related to food. When I have conducted week-long fasts during Holy Week, the persons who joined seemed to be exhilarated by their ability to refrain from solid food for five days. Some assumed they would be cowering in a corner, doubled over with pain. When we break the fast on Good Friday by eating a piece of fruit in silence, some feel a sense of sadness that the experience is ending.

I suspect that many people eat compulsively because they are trying to fill the hunger of their soul with food. At times we need to be physically hungry to be in touch with the deeper hunger of our soul. Little wonder that through the ages sages have turned to fasting for deeper spiritual concentration. They were able to use it to become reunited with their natural hunger for God beneath all their other cravings.

If you want to try a fast, don't do it alone. Invite members of your congregation to join you. A tremendous amount of bonding can happen around this shared experience. The groups I have led meet for two hours at the beginning of the fast and two hours at the break of the fast. I usually ask people to keep a journal throughout the five days, and when we get together at the end of the week, I ask them to share with one another the demons they wrestled with during their fast. The sense of communion is marvelous.

Practical Tips

There are several kinds of fasts. I recommend a juice fast which means suspending all solid food and limiting one's intake to selected juices. Avoid the fruit juices with heavy amounts of salt or sugar. Apple juice is the most popular for a fast because the pectin can temporarily relieve hunger pangs. It's also a good idea to drink lots of water because this helps the body's cleansing process. Hot water with a little lemon juice can be quite fulfilling.

During a fast, watching television may be difficult. If you do watch, you'll be amazed at how much our lives are manipulated by food ads.

It's important to begin and end a fast gently. In the twenty-four hours before a fast begins, restrict your diet to fruits and vegetables. Do the same in the twenty-four hours after breaking a fast. There is a growing bibliography on fasting; I've listed several sources in the notes for this chapter.[12]

Somatic Spirituality (Body Prayer)

"Somatic spirituality" is a phrase I use to consolidate those disciplines that involve body movement. Some people find body movement their most direct channel to the Holy. Yet all of us have been influenced by the Greeks, who tended to elevate the mind and soul over the body. This mind-body split continues to permeate our thinking. Classic Christian worship in western society encourages people to come to church, place their bodies in a pew, and worship God from the neck up. The German word for "squirming" is "rutching." How clearly I remember my mother admonishing me in church, "Kein rutching." In her theology, there was no such thing as a holy wiggle.

African-American worship as well as charismatic and Pentecostal worship are an exception to this neck-up kind of approach. In these churches, singing hymns while rocking sideways and waving one's arms is permitted, even expected. Sacred dance has had marginal acceptance in mainline churches, but it is usually regarded as a performance, not something the whole congregation can engage in.

Yet I continually hear from runners, swimmers, walkers, cyclists that their most profound prayer time is when they are moving. This certainly is true for me. Several years ago I had a type of conversion experience halfway through a ninety-minute run. One of the reasons I developed a positive addiction to running was the feeling that God spoke to me more often on a run than at any other time. Sometimes this worried me, and God and I have had many conversations about it: *Okay, God, what am I going to do when I become injured or too old to run anymore? Will You become manifest at other times that will be as intimate as when I was running?*

Those who report spiritual feelings as a result of body movement are usually people who stay with their activity for an hour or more. As George Sheehan, the guru of running types, says in *Running And Being*, the first thirty minutes is for your body, the following thirty minutes is for your soul.

Let's consider some other religions that use a somatic spirituality. Many Native American tribes use dance to invoke the gods, as do several African tribes. The Sufi tradition, the mystical wing of Islam, uses dance as their main form of worship, and it is a beautiful thing to witness. This tradition also contains the whirling dervish practice, which those who practice it claim brings them great ecstasy. The whirling dervishes in Old Testament times were condemned as heathens by the prophets. The dervishes used to spin themselves into ecstasy and then deliver a prophecy to the community.

The one Christian community indigenous to North America that practiced somatic Christianity is the Shakers. This religious movement did not believe in procreation, so their worship habits have been lost to our contemporary culture. Shakers used to dance or shake the whole night, men on one side of the room, women on the other. The artwork depicting these dance forms frequently shows someone writhing on the floor, supposedly in spiritual ecstasy.

Tai Chi, a movement meditation used by the Chinese, is beautiful to watch. Because the movements are made with such precision, the practice becomes a type of meditation as the participant focuses all attention on each sequence.

Hatha yoga would also in fit this category of spirituality. In the practice of hatha yoga, all the major muscles of the body are stretched and held for a count of nine. This keeps the body loose and flexible. The yogis say you are as young as your spine is flexible. The various stretching postures called asanas stimulate a release of certain emotions or spiritual insights.

In comparison, we can see how cerebral we are in the West in our religious expression. For some of you, however, body movement of some sort will become your path to the holy. Neurolinguistic programming would say that each of has a preference for how we take in data or remember things:

1. audio
2. visual
3. kinesthetic

To test which one you prefer, try to remember what you were doing last Monday evening. Do you remember sounds (such as the timbre of someone's voice)? Or do you recall a picture of yourself in some scene? Or do you re-experience the physical sensations you had that evening? If you remembered by re-experiencing the feelings and sensations of that evening, then you are primarily a kinesthetic person.

Some clergy use a particular sacred word or phrase once they get into a rhythmic body movement, such as Jesus is Lord, Kyrie eleison (Lord, have mercy), or Praise God from whom all blessings flow. I find that often a word or phrase will rise naturally in me at certain times of rhythmic body movement—pedalling a stationary bike, swimming laps, or running. I will listen to it for a while and become curious as to why that phrase is emerging from my psyche. Whenever the phrase or word is not particularly uplifting, such as "Diamonds are a girl's best friend," I deliberately choose another phrase to replace it.

For those of you who are kinesthetic types, somatic spirituality may be your pathway to prayer. If that is the case, how can you give more priority to body movement four or five days a week? Your life will feel a whole lot more balanced when you do.

Retreats/Days of Silence

More and more clergy are scheduling a private overnight retreat for themselves at a local monastery or retreat center several times a year. These times of prayer and reflection are not counted as vacation days or days for continuing education; these are extended periods in which pastors can enter into silence before God, to pray for themselves and their congregations. Introverts seem more drawn to this kind of spiritual discipline than Extravert personality types. When Introverts get some quality time away to be by themselves, they usually have much more to offer others when they return. Introverts can make great preachers, but they do require quality time alone to produce those sermons.

After midlife, Extraverts usually begin to sense the need for greater exploration of their inner life. Even Extraverts, who get their energy from interacting with lots of people, can run dry at times and need some alone time to feed their soul. They can see the benefit of going away to a place of solitude for a time of reading, prayer, walking, thinking, journal keeping, etc.

Observing the Daily Office

Some clergy gain a great deal by observing a daily office: Matins, Compline, etc. Clergy who are more structured and ordered tend to find this practice helpful. In the course of praying the office around the church calendar, they are able to systematically pray all of the Psalms. Even when they don't feel like observing this discipline, the routine of it keeps them at it. The Psalms take on new life for these clergy. Their knowledge of Scripture tends to broaden as well.

New Age Religion

Recently I have heard some who claim that anything that smacks of New Age religion is of the devil and should definitely be shunned. I am both saddened and distressed by this accusation. It feels as though New Age religion is the new straw man on whom we can project all our fears and against whom we can react. According to some of the anti-New Age folks, even something as basic as sitting quietly and listening to one's breath is considered Buddhist and therefore akin to worshipping foreign gods. Included in this accusation would be some of the spiritual disciplines I've advocated here such as chanting and meditation.

Don't get me wrong. There is much within the New Age religious movement that I consider far-out and hokey. But what gets lost in all the rhetoric and finger pointing is the fact that many people on this continent who have not expressed much interest in religion in the past are now genuinely interested in spiritual things. Is it possible to nurture that curiosity and gently lead people into practices that might have more substance for them? The New Age movement can be seen as a failure on the part of the churches in North America to address people's spiritual hunger. Perhaps we learn something from people who are attracted to New Age spirituality. Can we be open to hearing what needs seem to be addressed by New Age practices, needs that are not being met in our churches?

One of the things that is appealing about some New Age practices is their advocacy of wholistic health. Some emphasize healthy diets, body movement, and positive thinking. I am convinced that a Christian community could have the same appeal if it offered wholistic health-related programs.

I'm for being less judgmental about New Age practices and more open to hearing what they are saying about religion in our day and age. How can we be so sure where the Spirit is leading these days? I imagine that the Scribes and Pharisees would have considered the teaching and practice of Jesus as a sign of New Age religion and thus condemned it. We might also contemplate the saying of Jesus in John 10:16, "And I have other sheep that are not of this fold; I must bring them also and they will heed my voice. So there shall be one flock, one shepherd." Let's leave the judgment of who are sheep and who are goats up to God and know that we will be surprised at who ultimately shows up in that final fold.

* * * *

The first of our self-care strategies, the Spiritual Uplift, has really been a whole cornucopia of strategies. It is up to each of us to find the disciplines and practices that suit our personality type, our lifestyle, our metabolism, and our theology and to give them priority in our lives. Ministry will happen best for us when we are healthy on all three fronts: physical, emotional, and spiritual. For me, wholistic health begins with spiritual health, and spiritual health then informs and directs the other two. It is God's desire that we return to a state of wholeness, and God, in his or her wisdom, has provided many schemes for getting us there. I hope you will try some of these disciplines on for size. An adventure awaits you.

CHAPTER 13

Letting-Go Techniques

Techniques for letting go are geared toward reversing the effects of the fight/flight response to novel or threatening situations. Armed with one of these techniques, you can diffuse the destructive effects of stress on your body, mind, and spirit. Having a workable letting-go technique under your belt is like having good solid downspouting on your house. There is no way you can stop rain from drenching your home. But you can channel that rain through downspouts so that it doesn't do damage to the foundation or the flower beds.

Some of the best letting-go techniques are meditation, biofeedback, autogenic training, and hatha yoga. Because we have discussed the discipline of meditation under the heading of spiritual disciplines, I will proceed with the remaining three.

Biofeedback

As the term suggests, a mechanical device provides the individual with information on his/her biological functioning. One biofeedback instrument you've probably heard of is the electrocardiogram. An EKG provides the physician with some basic information on the heart's functioning. Patients who are allowed to either hear or see their own EKG may be alarmed at first that their heart appears to be beating so wildly. Over time, however, they realize that their heartbeat fluctuates considerably. What is more, they can begin to experiment with various kinds of relaxation exercises designed to lower the heartbeat.

The electroencephalograph (EEG) was one of the earlier biofeedback mechanisms used in stress reduction. This device measures the length and speed of a person's brain waves. Our normal brain waves, in a state called *beta*, are short and staccato. The EEG can detect when a person's brain waves move from a state of beta to *alpha*: the brain waves become longer and slower. The alpha state is accompanied by a feeling of deep peacefulness. I recall being hooked up to an EEG at a stress seminar and watching impatiently for the light to come on indicating I had reached the alpha state. The light didn't come on until I had relaxed by repeating the Lord's Prayer over and over again. I believe that "the peace that passes understanding" is an alpha state that happens to someone who, no matter what the external circumstance, throws themself completely upon the Grace of God. Those of us who preach this kind of peace need to experience it more often ourselves.

A far less expensive biofeedback mechanism is a small hand-held device that measures the skin's resistance to an electrical current. This is called a Galvanic Skin Response. When a person is nervous or anxious, s/he tends to perspire and the GSR picks it up. The polygraph machine or lie detector operates on the same principle.

Through the use of bio-feedback mechanisms, we can teach ourselves to control body temperature, pulse, blood pressure, and brain waves. Once we've learned the patterns and sensations, we can accomplish the same thing without the equipment.

My favorite biofeedback mechanism is called a Bio-Dot.[1] It is so inexpensive ($9.75 per hundred—about a dime a piece) that I invite people to wear them while attending one of my seminars. Bio-Dots are encapsulated crystals that change color depending upon hand temperature:

black—very tense
amber—tense
yellow—unsettled
green—involved (normal)
turquoise—relaxing
blue—calm
violet—very relaxed

I let participants know that as long as I am up front leading a session, my BioDot will be black. There is no way you can be giving leadership to a community and have your BioDot be blue. This explains why parishioners say, "Oh, your hands are cold!" when they shake hands with their pastors after Sunday worship. Those pastors have been under a lot of stress conducting worship, and if they were wearing a BioDot, it would be black.

Hand temperature is a very good indicator of one's level of stress. You will recall one of the things that happens when our mind triggers the fight/flight response is that the body, in its own economy, sends most of our blood to the large muscles of the body to prepare us for fighting or running. Under stress our body withdraws the blood from our hands to send it to our torso, biceps, etc. The minute the blood is withdrawn from our hands, the hand temperature drops and the BioDot turns black. When the stressful situation is over, the blood flows more normally to our hands and feet, and our BioDot moves slowly from yellow to green to a nice deep blue. I've decided our worship liturgies should add a final benediction with the versicle:

Preacher: "May your dot always be blue"
Congregation: "And also with you."

Autogenic Training

It surprises me that autogenic training has not caught on more dramatically in this country. It is a potent relaxation technique, yet unlike meditation which can have a kind of "eastern religion" stigma attached to it, autogenic training is a secular, scientific process. Other terms to describe autogenic training are auto-hypnosis or auto-suggestion.

In a sense, individuals using this practice are hypnotizing themselves. The founder of the practice, German psychiatrist Johannes H. Schultz, discovered that people can indeed hypnotize themselves when their objective is a pleasant, healthful state of relaxation. His research noted that clients who were able to accomplish this state had a substantial lessening of fatigue and tension as well as a reduction in the incidence and severity of psychosomatic disorders such as headaches.[2]

The process begins with the participant, eyes closed, assuming a comfortable position lying on the floor or sitting up straight in a chair. Beginning with the arm used most often, the individual repeats silently, "My right (or left) arm is heavy." This formula is repeated three to six times for thirty to sixty seconds. Then the individual opens his/her eyes and stirs rather vigorously. At this point, participants usually notice that their arm retains a sensation of heaviness. The exercise is repeated four times, allowing about a minute between each repetition. Then the focus shifts to the less active arm, and the same series is repeated. After each sequence of silent repetition of the phrases, it is important to cancel them out with movement and phrases such as, "eyes open, arms firm, breathe deeply." The same procedure is followed with each leg.

Once the "heaviness" series is complete, the practitioner then repeats the same series using the concept of warmth: "My right arm is warm." Schultz has noted that subjects in his research who entered the hypnotic trance state experienced two overwhelming physical sensations. One was a pleasurable feeling of generalized warmth throughout the body and the other a feeling of heaviness in the limbs and torso.

The next stage of the training involves the cardiovascular system. Practitioners learn to regulate their heartbeat by repeating the phrase, "Heartbeat calm and regular." Then the focus shifts to respiration. While practicing the first three exercises, most people notice a striking decrease in respiratory frequency and an increase in depth of respiration. To enhance this naturally occurring phenomenon, the individual focuses on his/her respiration and repeats the phrase, "It breathes me." The next exercise is intended to induce a sensation of warmth in the abdominal region—which tends to produce a calming effect on the central nervous system. The formula used to achieve this is, "My solar plexus is warm."

Finally, the last stage in autogenic training involves the use of the phrase, "My forehead is cool." This has a way of calming the mind.

After two months to a year, these six initial stages of autogenic training can be done very quickly, between two to four minutes for the entire sequence. Picture a high-powered executive having come through a brutal morning of bite-the-bullet decisions. At a break in the day, this executive tells the secretary to hold all calls, lies down on the floor, and within two to four minutes, has moved into a deeply relaxing trance. At the end of ten minutes, the executive returns to the stress of the day, having experienced the equivalent of a two-hour nap. This is the potential of autogenic training. It may take four to six months to learn the process through discipline and practice, but once learned, we can move quickly to deeply relaxing states during which the destructive effects of stress are reversed and the fight/flight response has been turned on its head.

One of the advantages of autogenic training is that it begins with easily understandable and easily learned exercises and then moves to more advanced and esoteric stages. The advanced practitioner can gain control over his/her autonomic system for self-healing and can reach profound states of relaxation in which they are highly attuned to unconscious symbolism and fantasies. By interacting with their unconscious minds, they can solve problems or confront deeply internal issues.

As with meditation, beginners can benefit by merely following the "skeleton" instructions, but it is helpful to practice with others and to share experiences. With qualified instructors, participants can go deeper much more quickly. If autogenic training is offered through your local hospital or stress center, consider signing up. It may be the letting-go technique that suits your temperament, your lifestyle, and your metabolism.

Hatha Yoga

Some people need to engage in some sort of body movement in order to reach states of relaxation. This may explain the increased popularity of the practice of hatha yoga. There are few video exercise series that do not utilize some of the stretches and movements of hatha yoga.

Rather than placing hatha yoga in the category of eastern religious practice, I have come to see it as the science of systematically stretching every major muscle in the body for purposes of health and relaxation. At Alban Institute's ten-day Clergy Development Institute we engage participants in an hour-long pre-breakfast time of hatha yoga, singing, chanting, and meditating. It's not surprising that many of these participants report continuing the discipline once they return to their places of ministry. Having experienced the physical rejuvenation of these body movements, they want to continue tapping into this source of vitality.

When you stretch a muscle and hold that stretch for six to nine seconds, the elasticity of the muscles is retained. From about age eighteen on, our muscles become shorter and tighter and we gradually lose flexibility and elasticity. This often leads to injury because our muscles tear rather than stretch when strained abnormally.

Picture an older person, hunched over, barely able to turn his head sideways. Some of this may be due to arthritis, but much can also be a result of inactivity. Hatha yoga would say that we either use our muscles or we lose them. Yoga practitioners say that you are as young as your spine is flexible. About ten to fifteen minutes of yoga stretches three times a week is enough to keep the major muscles in the body loose and limber.[3]

Here's to a healthier, more flexible you!

CHAPTER 14

Time Out

The research on burnout generally agrees that chronic fatigue and apathy develop from being overly committed and involved in our work. The literature on stress states that there are only so many life changes that we can endure. A clear coping srtategy is to remove ourselves from an agitated, changing environment and take some time for ourselves. Yet, because the role of religious authority is often ambiguous, we clergy have difficulty knowing when we have done enough and can take time for ourselves. It often seems more prudent to do "just one more thing" before taking time out.

We need to figure out our own rhythms of rest and be true to them. In order to function well in the clergy role over the long haul, we need to take regular time for ourselves:

- on a daily basis
- on a weekly basis
- on a quarterly basis
- on a yearly basis
- on a sabbatical basis (every four years)

Daily Breaks

For most of us, our ministry gets the first cut of our energy, our family the next cut of energy, and anything left goes to ourselves. If there is no energy left over at the end of the day, we go without blessing ourselves in some concrete way. Single clergy sometimes try to make the parish their family so all of their time goes to the church with no time left for themselves or their friends.

To combat this inevitable energy crunch, clergy who engage in healthy self-care practices build in something just for themselves at the front end of the day. Even those who are not morning people have a plan for squeezing something into their day that gives them the shot in the arm they need.

Just imagine you had twenty-five hours per day to work with. What would you do with the extra hour each day if it were given to you as a gift? Most of us know intuitively what such activity we would choose. The trick is to really make the time for it, so that it can begin to nourish us.

"Sorry to interrupt the vacation, folks. Your congregation has called ~~the ranger station~~ twenty-eight times to say they can't find the communion glasses."

Weekly Breaks

It has always struck me as strange that all the other professions allow two days off per week, while the norm for clergy is one day off per week. Because clergy are working on Sundays, they don't get a day of rest like other people. They spend their Saturdays doing what everyone else does Saturdays: mowing the lawn, doing the laundry, getting the car fixed, getting a haircut, cleaning the house. Clergy miss those Sundays of visiting friends or having leisurely meals or going for a walk. Clergy can't expect to stay vital in the ministry for long if they don't have this "Sunday" time.

For this reason, I strongly recommend the spiritual discipline of Sabbath time. How easily we dismiss God's fourth commandment: "Six days you shall labor and the seventh YOU SHALL REST." We do some crazy mental flips and talk about keeping the Sabbath in spirit through worship, while forgetting the logic and wisdom behind the need for regular weekly rest for both physical and spiritual renewal. We could well learn from our Jewish brothers and sisters that we need not only a day of rest, but a day to prepare for Sabbath. In other words, I am recommending that we learn to help our parishes flourish on five days a week.

Sunday cannot be your Sabbath. If you preach every Sunday, you expend as much psychic energy in three hours on Sunday morning as in a ten-hour day. Your Sabbath needs to be on a Tuesday or a Friday, or some other day than Sunday. I would recommend scheduling two consecutive days off per week because for some of you it is too difficult to relax when you have important events happening the next day. Two days off in a row gives you one unpressured day out of your clergy role.

I believe each of us can learn to do our ministries in a fifty-hour work week. That is still ten hours more per week than many persons work. With good time management, we are giving the parish five ten-hour days and that's a lot. We need a new set of heroes among the clergy. We need persons who can make a church come alive without sacrificing their bodies, their families, or their souls. As I've said earlier, when we work more than fifty hours per week, one of three things tends to go awry in our lives: 1) our bodies deteriorate because there is not enough time to rest, exercise, or eat properly, 2) our relational life goes because there is no quality time with significant others, or 3) our spiritual life suffers because there is not enough time to read, journal, walk, think, pray, etc.

But, you may argue, don't our parishioners work their full week and then volunteer their free time to work in the church? Shouldn't we be volunteering some of our free time to the church as well? Yes, you may volunteer some of your time to the church, but not to your own parish. We need to recognize the qualitative difference between what people do when they volunteer and what they do on their job. Our volunteer work is an outlet for us, something we do that helps us grow, be with people we like, or contribute to projects we care about. The church is doing people a favor by offering them volunteer opportunities, which can bring meaning and significance to their lives. But when you as the clergy person do anything at your church you are in the role of the religious authority. That is work. You can only work so long at a job before it begins to go sour on you.

Think of the vitality your ministry would have if you really did have a Sabbath day each week. This would be a qualitatively different time than the other six days. Six days a week you would work to manipulate your environment for the better. On the seventh you would enjoy every-thing just as it is. On your Sabbath day, you might look out at your lawn, recognizing that it needed to be cut, yet also recognizing that it is perfect just the way it is. The pile of laundry in the corner—perfect. That neighbor who is screwed up—time to just enjoy him for what he is.

Jesus chided the Scribes and the Pharisees for their legalism in regard to the Sabbath, but he did not do away with a day of rest. The Sabbath is a wonderful spiritual discipline that is built right in to the order of creation. In six days God created the world, and on the seventh God rested. How much of the craziness of our lives would fall away if we would return to Sabbath observance? How healing it would be for us and what a wonderful model for our parishioners in coping with the madness of their lives.

Quarterly Breaks

Most people on this continent enjoy periodic long weekends. So should clergy. When was the last time, other than during your vacation time, that you had a long weekend to yourself? Some congregations offer their pastor one weekend a quarter away from the parish that is not counted as vacation time. Simply being relieved of Sunday morning responsibilities once a quarter is a real break.

Yearly Breaks

Each year you will need time to get out from under caring for people non-stop. Even when you are supposed to be having some time off, people don't stop having problems, and when they do, they want their pastor around. Few lay people are aware of this constant pressure and sometimes begrudge clergy their month's vacation each year. I continually find clergy who do not take their full vacation each year. Many have fallen into the practice of returning from their vacation when an influential parishioner dies. It's as though it is a sign of non-caring when we do not return to work when people die. When we have a medical emergency, we are usually only too happy to see another doctor when our own is on vacation. Why is it different with clergy?

I know this issue of availability during crises produces anxiety for many clergy. Possibly it's because those clergy who went before us set a bad precedent in the parish. It would be great if someone from our denomination would come in and set matters straight on this issue and others like it. Unfortunately, that probably won't happen. Part of our job is to teach our congregations how they can better care for their clergy. Congregations that support their clergy will have fewer pastoral difficulties, while congregations that wring their clergy dry, yet pay them minimum salary and give them little time away, generally have more problems. If we don't take the time we need for our own sake, let's do it for the sake of our successors in the parish. We need to be systematically teaching our congregations how they can support clergy health and vitality. Establishing some healthier norms for parish emergencies when clergy are on vacation is a good place to start.

Sabbaticals

It is ludicrous to think we can continue to be fresh, vital, and relevant year after year in parish ministry without taking some extended periods of time away for renewal and refreshment. The quality of your sermons will be better if you take a three-month sabbatical every four years.

Alban Institute's research on the Long Pastorate (ten years or more in one place) convinced me of the need for clergy sabbaticals. In this study, clergy interviewed members of their congregations on their chief concerns about long pastorates. The top concern was that the clergy person would become stale and "go to seed." At the same time we discovered that the burnout scores for clergy in a long pastorate were considerably higher than for clergy who change pastorates more frequently.

What's the formula for keeping a congregation on its growing edge in a long pastorate? I recommend hiring a consultant to assist the congregation in a planning process every four to five years. At the end of that planning process the pastor should be encouraged to go on a sabbatical. Clergy in long pastorates burn out because the longer they are in place, the more responsibility they seem to accumulate. A sabbatical is one way to break that pattern. When the congregation has set a new direction with a long-range plan, and the pastor is away for a three-month sabbatical, it's important that s/he not pick up all the old responsibilities upon returning. It's almost as if you're starting a new pastorate while remaining in the same place.

The bright folk in the parish know it is in their self-interest to offer a competent pastor a periodic sabbatical. If their pastor remains vital in the ministry, the parish avoids the difficult task of finding and calling a new pastor after the old one has burned out. In most denominations, it takes twelve to eighteen months for the search process and then it takes another two to three years for a new pastor to get to know the parish and get things moving. With each pastoral transition, the congregation loses about two to three years of effective pastoral care. That is not a very efficient way to run a parish. It is in their self interest to give their current pastor a four-month sabbatical and have him/her return with vitality to take them on another growth spurt.

If we go to our congregations with hat in hand asking for a sabbatical as if they would be doing us a favor, we are going with the wrong attitude. A sabbatical is not a vacation. It is for their sake as well as yours that you go on a sabbatical. The Alban publication *Learning to Share the Ministry*[1], by James R. Adams and Celia A. Hahn, is a story of one parish that got as much out of their pastor's sabbatical as he did. This congregation loved their pastor and wanted to support his sabbatical by organizing themselves into committees to take on all his pastoral roles. They learned the areas in which they really did need someone at the center of the parish to hold it all together. Further, they learned how complex the pastor's role was, and yet how fulfilling as well. The group that volunteered to visit those who were sick in the hospital did not give up that role when the pastor returned. The pastor came back to a new role in the parish. I recommend that clergy give this book to some of their lay leaders to get them excited about what might be in store for them during their pastor's sabbatical. The Alban publication *Sabbatical Planning,* by Richard Bullock, can also assist you in this self-care strategy.[2]

CHAPTER 15

Support Systems That Work

A pastor once described his job this way: "I feel like a chunk of cheese from which everyone wants just a nibble." When we lose control of our lives in this way, we need strong support in order to get our lives back. It will mean saying "no" to people, which will upset both them and us. Few of us can do this without a group of people behind us to support us. Most of us underestimate our vulnerability and, when the confrontation comes, we fold. As we start to fold, we need people to say, "Look, what you're doing for yourself is very important. You need to hang in there with this commitment to yourself. Now is not the time to be backing down from your decision to limit your involvement in certain activities in the parish."

Support systems are also vital to us when things become unusually stressful in our lives. When we have too much change, flux, and novelty in our lives, we're thrown off balance. A support system can be an anchor in a windstorm. Members of our support group have probably experienced something similar to what we're going through and can offer perspective. For example, being surprised by an income tax audit is certainly an adjustment, but the edge can be taken off when we can talk to others who have been through that ordeal.

Research on people who have been through life crises reaffirms the importance of support systems. Social scientist Eric Lindemann talked to a number of survivors of the devastating Cocoanut Grove fire in which 129 people were killed. He discovered that those survivors who had lots of human contact and socio-emotional support managed to recover quickly, some of them rising to a level of self-esteem and well-being they had not known prior to the incident. Most of these people had not received in-depth therapy or counseling. They simply had people who called or dropped by to check on how they were doing. Some of this human contact may have seemed superficial to the outside observer, yet in the midst of a crisis it was amazingly therapeutic. The survivors who had little or no positive human contact, however, had a long and difficult recovery, some of them never really making a comeback from the tragedy.[1]

Having strong social support may also help us live longer. In a nine-year study of 7,000 persons in Alameda County, California, Aaron Antonovsky, professor at Ben Gurion University in Israel, discovered that people with many social ties (marriage, close friendships, extended families, church membership, or group associations) had a far lower mortality rate than those who lacked quality or depth in their social support systems. A similar study by Lisa Berkman, an epidemiologist now at Yale University, supports this finding: she found that men in their fifties, who are at high risk because of a very low social and economic status, but who score high on an index of social networks, lived far longer than high status men with low social network scores.[2] The evidence is substantial: the higher the quality of our support network, the longer we will live and the more effectively we will confront change, trauma, or tragedy in our lives.

How Support Systems Work in a Church Context

Most of us don't need much more convincing about the importance of quality support networks in our lives. The problem is how to make them work given our particular, and peculiar, ministry roles. Many clergy have expressed to me considerable frustration in finding the kind of support they need. They wonder if it's right to turn to people in the parish for support. Can you befriend parishioners and still be their spiritual authority and guide? Is such a seeming hierarchy even necessary anymore? If you don't find personal support within the parish, where do you find it?

All of these questions have to do with the intricacies of the pastoral role and the nature of the ministry. For clergy, the most helpful support systems are those that allow them to be "out of role" for a time. The Oscillation Theory, developed by Bruce Reed of the Grubb Institute, helps explain why.[3] Reed describes two modes of life between which we need to oscillate if we are to remain healthy.

Doing	Being
Meeting the requirements of an achievement oriented culture	Accepting who and what we are

Work	Play
Energy expended towards the accomplishment of tasks and goals	The emergence of our "playful child" in certain "safe" environments

Role	Essence
The assumption of position vis-a-vis each other: i.e., president, janitor, salesman, etc., which permits institutions to function	Who we are; in the absence of our roles

Task Orientation	Sabbath Time
The manipulation of things and people for the accomplishment of goals	The acceptance and enjoyment of things and people just as they are

Law	Grace
The "shoulds" and "oughts" that move communal life from chaos to structure That which reminds us that we have not measured up to expectations	The good news that we are accepted just the way we are. We are loved. We are free.

All of these modes reflect either

Intra-dependence   or   **Extra-dependence**

A state in which I depend upon internal resources to accomplish tasks important to me. In this state I am autonomous and self- sufficient. I depend on resources inside of me (intra) in this state.	A state in which I am dependent upon a resource outside of me that I feel is trusting and caring therefore allowing me to play, experience my essence, experience Grace or Sabbath time, or to just BE.

The following graphic illustrates the motion of the oscillation.

Doing	Being
Work	Play
Role	Essence
Responsibility/Achievement	Sabbath Time
Law	Grace

Intra-Dependence   **Extra-Dependence**

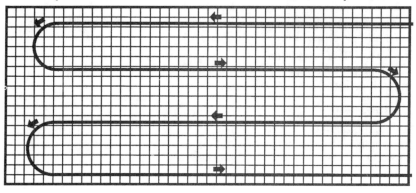

When we fail to oscillate between these two states, we tend to lose our perspective on reality. Often we can get stuck in Intra-dependence and become caught up in our roles and sense of responsibility. It's only when we move over to the Extra-dependence side that we catch glimpses of the madness and folly of our life. In Extra-dependence we can see much more clearly that we are taking ourselves, our roles, and responsibilities too seriously. Periodically we need to move into a state where we do not have to be in charge and can allow ourselves to be cared for.

Though they're often unconscious of it, people come to church to get their Extra-dependence needs met. They come from their world of Intra-dependence bruised, confused, disillusioned, in need of nurture and caring—even if for just a little while. The familiarity and trustworthiness of the pastor is key. Reed tells this story to illustrate Extra-dependence: In the middle of a service in a small parish in England, a woman fainted in the pew. The rector paused to see if others would respond to her needs. When they didn't, he stepped down from the chancel area and took care of the situation, getting those nearby to take her out for fresh air and a glass of water. As he pondered the incident later in the week, he was dumbfounded. Sitting in the pews that day were half a dozen doctors and nurses. It wasn't until the rector heard the oscillation theory that he understood that during the service those doctors and nurses were not in charge—he, the priest, was in charge. They were in a state of Extra-dependence. They trusted him to be able to manage the incident.

In one sense, we clergy are saying to people on a Sunday morning, "Listen, folks, you have been in charge all week, and you probably need a rest. Why not let me be in charge for awhile. So everybody sit down and relax your bodies. Let's sing a few hymns and do some familiar things together. And let me remind you how it is out there in the world. God is in charge of the universe, and God loves you, and I love you. Now get out of here." The following week they come back and say to you, "Listen pastor, you said that God was in control out there. It ain't so. That's a cutthroat world out there, and we've gotten badly bruised again." To which you respond, "Yes, I know. Never mind that right now. Let's relax and sing a few hymns and do some familiar things together. And before you go, let me remind you about some basics again. God is in control of this universe, and God loves you, and I love you. Now get out of here." That's a simple summary of how members oscillate in and out of Sunday morning worship.

The implications of this theory for clergy are enormous. All the while we are offering people Extra-dependence through either worship or pastoral care, we are in a state of Intra-dependence.

In addition to our role as provider of others' Extra-dependence, we are also the chief executive officer of a rather substantive operation. We bounce back and forth between being a leader/manager and the resident holy person. Both of those roles require that we be in a state of Intra-dependence. It raises the serious issue of where clergy can go for their Extra-dependence. Those places are few and far between for clergy. In fact, you may even have to pay for the opportunity to regress a bit.

Take a minute to reflect on the places to which you have access where you are able to get out of role, where other people manage the experience, or better yet, take personal care of you for awhile. Naturally, the first place we look is home and family. Hopefully, your home is a place where you can experience Extra-dependence some of the time. Yet, it cannot be that for you all of the time because significant others may also have some Extra-dependence needs they want you to fulfill. If we are married and have children, we have roles to fill—parent and spouse. If your spouse is employed outside the home, s/he may need you to take control for awhile so that s/he can "crash." It is unlikely that you can take care of everyone in the church and community and then come home and expect to be totally taken care of. Folks at home will soon feel exploited.

The most popular place for clergy to receive Extra-dependence is continuing education. It's our chance to go somewhere and have someone else be in charge for awhile. Returning to the seminary to listen to a lecture series by a popular figure allows us the opportunity to just BE. If we learn something useful to take back to our parish, so much the better. Depending on how much we need to be taken care of, we may resist being placed in small discussion groups. We may simply want to get lost in a large group for awhile so we can get some distance and perspective on our life and ministry.

When I do workshops around the country, I can provoke a good deal of anger if I don't take charge of the event and offer groups content, structure, and rituals by which they can feel taken care of. Clergy can become quite infantile in a retreat setting. They simply lose their sense of time and responsibility and want others to help them find their room and show them where the evening meal will be served. Yet given how completely clergy deplete themselves taking care of everyone else, this kind of regression should come as no surprise.

Spiritual direction and therapy are two ways clergy can receive Extra-dependence (see chapters 14 and 22 for more on these strategies). We could say that we are allowing our therapist or our spiritual director to be our pastor for awhile. In growing numbers, clergy are turning to convents, monasteries, or retreat centers for nurture and care. Spending a couple of days at a monastery is quite different from staying at home for rest. The experience of being provided with a clean room, three meals a day, and optional attendance at the daily mass is enough to allow many of us to feel taken care of.

I hope you have one or two solid friends with whom you can be completely out of role. For this reason, I discourage clergy from using parishioners to meet their Extra-dependence needs. This is not to say we should avoid having friendships in our parishes. In times of crisis we need to have some people we trust in the parish to see us through. But no matter how informal and friendly we are with a parishioner, it will be difficult to move completely into a state of Extra-dependence. From time to time, we will need to flip back into being their pastor. And at times when we least expect it, they may flip us back into role because they need something from us as clergy. In some cases, the role issues may become so complicated that the parishioner loses his "pastor." Conversely, I have heard some clergy talk about their feelings of loss when a close friend decides to join their church. They may have gained a good parishioner, but they have also lost a friend.

Being Intentional About Support Systems

A myth prevails about support systems. We continue to assume that a good support network happens by accident. We fail to see that quality support takes work. We need to sit down periodically and take stock of our support base. Do we have the kind of support relationships that will see us through what confronts us up ahead? Any work we do to upgrade the quality of our support network will pay off down the line, both personally and professionally.

Our support network needs to be varied enough to assist us in these dimensions of our life:

– **Our current ministry.** Do we have people who can give us the perspectives we need on all the issues facing us in our work?

– **Our personal life.** Do we have people who care deeply for us and what we are trying to do with our lives? Do we have people behind us who will see us through the emotional roller coaster on which the chances and changes of life will take us?

– **Our relational life.** Do we have people who care about our marriages and our relationship with our kids? If we are single, do we have people who support our consistently seeking out relationships that will be significant for us?

– **Our spiritual well-being.** Are there people who pray for us and who stand with us as we wrestle with the deeper issues of our lives?

Perhaps a brief exercise will give you some clues as to the breadth and depth of your current support network. Take a sheet of paper and write down all the names of the people who are your encouragers. These are the people who affirm you, who believe in what you are trying to do with your life, and who always leave you feeling good about yourself after you have spent time with them.

Got that list ready? Let's take some time to work with that list. Begin by circling the names of three people outside of your immediate family who would find a way to take three days off and spend time with you if something traumatic happened. Let's say your family was wiped out in an accident, or you just got fired from your church, or you just broke your back in an automobile accident. Who, outside your family system, would take that time to be with you? Got three names? One name? Have you been in contact with those persons in the last thirty days? The last question asks what kind of a supporter are you. Do you take the time to initiate contact with people important to you?

Next, draw a line through the names of people who are eliminated when answering the following four questions. This should give you a better idea of the depth and breadth of your support network.

1. Draw a line through all the people on that list who are in your immediate family—spouse, children, parents, brothers, sisters, aunts and uncles, grandparents. One reason for doing this is because we as clergy tend to overuse our family when it comes to support. Possibly this is because there are so few outside of our families whom we trust to understand our unique situation.

2. Now draw a line through all the people who live more than fifty miles away from you. Researchers have been able to document that we tend to use less frequently those supporters who live at a distance from us. To contact them usually means a long distance phone call. If our telephone bill has been high lately, we think twice about calling and talking with a friend for an hour. And if seeing him or her requires driving for an hour or two, we may decide against it if we're very tired and depressed.

3. The third group to take off your list are all the people who are in your denomination. This question often wipes out people's lists. Yet I firmly believe that if all of your support is coming from one system, you are very vulnerable. Thousands of pastors leave the parish ministry every year. Who will be your supporters if you leave that role? Some of your friends within your denomination will not forsake you if you leave the

ministry, but it will be hard for you to stay connected with them because the usual ways you interact will be gone.

4. The last people to take off the list are all ordained persons, regardless of denomination. We clergy do tend to flock together and build bonds of friendship. There are times, however, when you need a lay perspective on life. Your relationship with other clergy will also come to an end if you ever move or leave the ordained ministry.

Do you still have some people on your list? Most clergy in the workshops I lead have only one or two left on their list. Over seventy-five percent of the names are wiped out completely. I hope this exercise will give you ideas about how to broaden the support base in your life. This will require hard, intentional work, but it will help you sustain your emotional stability in a very volatile profession.

Peer Support Groups

I have been encouraging clergy to think about a peer support group with a paid facilitator as a means of meeting their Extra-dependence needs. Such a group would be different from most of the kinds of groups we've been a part of that don't work. In the absence of strong leadership at the center of most groups, the trust level usually doesn't develop and meetings get reduced to "bitch and brag" sessions. I don't want to minimize the usefulness of catching up on the gossip of the denomination or the community or having a place to complain about how awful things are or what wonderful things we were able to do last Sunday. But having a support group where the trust is high and where we can share our pain and vulnerability is worth its weight in gold. The reason I believe in having a paid facilitator comes right out of the theory of oscillation: No one moves easily to a state of Extra-dependence until they perceive strength and caring at the center of the experience. In short, we need to hire someone to be a pastor to us when we gather as peers to review our lives.

What I am advocating is a dependence model of support. It works so much better than groups that try to go it on their own, providing their own leadership. It's good to remember some of the prerequisites of

Extra-dependence, e.g., familiarity, predictability, strength, and caring. Leadership in a peer support group is not very predictable when the role of leader is passed around from one member to another. And, if one person in the group regularly provides leadership that's familiar and predictable, when does that person get to enter into Extra-dependence?

I contend that any clergy support group that has high trust and candor has found one or two persons in the group that they can lean on to manage their Extra-dependence. And probably that group is unaware of how much they are depending on those individuals, or how much it is diminishing the experience of nurture for those leaders. I believe it's better to acknowledge these needs from the beginning and contract for that kind of leadership up front. It's best to pay the person to keep the role clear and clean.

It's a gift to be able to come panting into a trusted group of peers and have someone take charge and say, "Let's spend a few minutes in silence to get ourselves totally here, and then let's each take five minutes to share the highs and lows of our week." You're not asking the facilitator to do the group's loving or confronting. With a gifted facilitator, however, participants are able to let their feelings about one another hang out there. They can trust that the facilitator is paying attention to what's happening, to who's getting too much of something and not enough of something else. It's hard work managing a group in which people are letting their pain and vulnerability show, and these people should be compensated in some way.

The following is one way I would recommend going about structuring this kind of peer support group for yourself:

1. Think about one clergy colleague in your area with whom you would feel free to share your pain and vulnerability. If you find yourself resisting the thought of sharing with this person some failure or embarrassment in your personal or professional life, you may need to find someone else. Once you have found this one person, ask to have lunch with her or him and describe the concept of peer support groups above. If you get a positive response, move on to step 2.

2. Between the two of you, think of three or four other individuals with whom the two of you would feel free to share your pain and vulnerability. This is no time to be pastoral to other clergy in the area. If you know some fellow pastor is hurting and could use such a support group,

yet you also know that his or her presence in your group would destroy the trust level for you, then don't ask that person. Find some other way to minister to that pastor's need. At this point you need to go after that quality of support that will render you more effective as a pastor. You need to select members of that group carefully and well.

3. Decide between the two of you who will be a the group facilitator for your peer support group. Remember, this person will need three qualitities. He or she will need to be competent, sensitive, and safe. He or she will need to be competent at group management and development, sensitive to the complexities of parish ministry, and in no way able to influence your career path in the church. (Certain judicatory officials will not do as group facilitators; you probably would not feel safe sharing points of failure in your ministry with persons who are part of your church hierarchy.) When you have settled on a facilitator, decide what you will pay this person to perform this task. A quality support group should be worth some money to its participants. Sometimes middle judicatories will have some scholarship funds for this purpose for each church executive knows his/her clergy need more support. If such funds are not available, clergy should feel free to use their continuing education money for this purpose.

4. Be sure also to agree upon the time at which the group experience will be evaluated. All of us can be anxious about committing ourselves to a group when we don't know how long it will run, or how we can express our dissatisfaction should it not suit our needs.

Desired Change

CHAPTER 16

Getting the Body Moving

The lack of physical exercise is considered by doctors to be the most serious health hazard among North Americans. This includes our children. We have all become so sedentary that we are jeopardizing our health.

In 1989, the Center for Disease Control in Atlanta reported that at least five of the eleven physical fitness goals set in 1980 would not be met by 1990. The Center has been able to document that regular physical exercise reduces the incidence of many medical conditions—and most notably aids in fighting heart disease, colon cancer, diabetes, and obesity. Yet, overall, we are not participating in regular physical activity.

According to aerobic specialists, we need at least twenty minutes of exercise three times a week to keep our cardiovascular systems healthy. During these exercise periods, we need to increase our heart rate to about 120 beats per minute. We may need additional exercise to keep our weight in check or develop muscle tone, but those sessions of heavy breathing are the minimum for cardiovascular fitness.

When we don't exercise vigorously three or four times a week our hearts become weak and have to work much harder to get the blood through our system. When we exercise vigorously our hearts become stronger, so that our resting pulse rate drops significantly. Before I developed a running regimen, my resting pulse ranged from eighty to ninety beats a minute. After several years of running three to four miles a day three days a week, my resting pulse dropped to between fifty and sixty beats per minute. It's hard to imagine, but my heart beats thirty fewer times per minute or 1800 beats fewer times per hour since I've engaged in a regular exercise program. That adds up to 43,200 beats per day. If our heart has only so many beats in a lifetime, it stands to reason that we might last longer if we exercise regularly.

The important element in exercise is regularity. A two-hour tennis game every two weeks won't do the trick. We need sports activities that will engage us vigorously, yet unless we are able to arrange these several times a week, we need to supplement them with another aerobic exercise.

The Research on Exercise and Health

The research confirms the important effect of exercise on our health and longevity. Moderate exercise dramatically boosts chances of survival for people with high blood pressure, suggests an eight-year study reported in *USA Today*.[1]

Exercise also helps lower blood pressure, which reduces the risk of stroke and heart attack, according to a study by Dr. Larry Gibbons. "If you have hypertension, you can stack the odds of staying alive much more in your favor by getting moderately fit," says Dr. Larry Gibbons, medical director of the Cooper Clinic in Dallas.[2] A similar study by Dr. Lars Ekelund of Duke University Medical Center in Durham, North Carolina, found that the least fit among 3,106 men were 4.3 times more likely to die of heart attack.

A study begun in the mid-1950s with 250,000 Armed Forces veterans is showing that men's risk of certain cancers is strongly tied to how much physical labor their jobs demand. The more exercise, the lower the risk of dying from colon, brain, and kidney cancer and leukemia.

Regular exercise is also one of the best ways to counter the effects of aging, according to studies by the American Physical Therapy Association, Geriatrics Section. The person who exercises regularly is stimulating bone and muscle tissue and keeping them strong and flexible. The heart and lungs also benefit substantially from regular exercise.

The research should convince us clergy to change our ways, but it hasn't. The July 1987 Pastoral Ministry Newsletter reported on a survey of parish clergy. Of those clergy between the ages of thirty-five and fifty:

— ninety-four percent had no defined physical fitness program,
— seventy-eight percent were overweight by sixteen pounds or
  more, and
— eighty-nine percent admitted to poor eating habits.

Why don't we do what we know is good for us? Lots of reasons,
not the least of which is simple inertia. Somehow we have to believe
that getting over that initial hump will be worth it.

The Redemption Workout

It is a cold November evening as I return to my motel room after an
exhausting day of leading forty clergy through an eight-hour training
module. My throat feels like it's bleeding. My legs are stiff and sore
from standing up in front of people all day. I strip off my suit and fall on
the bed. Its 6:30 p.m.

What to do? What I feel like doing is simply going to bed and
sleeping, yet wisdom tells me that I will awaken at 2:00 a.m. and won't
be able to get back to sleep. My other inclination is to go down to the
hotel restaurant and have a couple of drinks and a big meal. I reject this
idea as well because I know the self-criticism I will engage in when I
indulge myself with heavy food after a basically sedentary day. The
room television advertises several movies available for a price. Several
of the descriptions are made to sound sensual and inviting. Several X-
rated skin flicks are also available. In the privacy of my room, who will
censor me? Yet I'm aware that this alternative will not lead to a whole
lot of peace of mind by the end of the evening. What to do?

I call down to the switchboard to see if there is a health spa connected to the hotel. The pleasant voice tells me that although they don't
have a facility on site, they do have an arrangement with a neighboring
hotel. By sheer will I force myself into comfortable jogging clothes and
walk downstairs. My body tells me I am crazy.

As I enter the spa I'm impressed with both the variety of equipment
and how empty it is. The only Nautilus machine that I think I can
manage with my low energy is the exercycle. I sit heavily on the seat,
leaning on the handlebars, and start my legs pedaling. It doesn't feel
good at all. I think I have made a mistake and decide I will only work

out for ten minutes and then collapse in the sauna. I keep my legs moving and listen to my breath start to labor and feel the moisture begin to form on my forehead.

Two other people walk into the spa, and one takes up the other exercycle beside me. He turns out to be a born-again Christian who is on fire about his local church. His enthusiasm is contagious, and I allow myself to ride with his energy. At the end of ten minutes of conversation and pedalling I peel down to my tee shirt and punch in another ten-minute program (Nautilus exercyles have computer programs that simulate pedalling through valleys and hills. You can choose from fifteen different levels of difficulty.)

At the end of fifty minutes, I finally leave the exercycle and go to the rowing machine. My energy is building. I notice how pleased I am with my decision to go the workout route this evening. While vigorously exercising, I am processing the day and finding myself getting excited about some things I plan to do with the group in the morning. After twenty minutes on the rowing machine and another fifteen minutes lifting weights, I finally do get to the pool and sauna. By this time I am feeling exhilarated and grateful. What a wonderful body God has given me! It has been the means to the experience of Grace more often than anything else I can think of. I recall a line from the movie "Chariots of Fire." The missionary youth is responding to his girlfriend who is trying to get him to give up on the Olympics and go straight to seminary: "God has made me fast. When I run, I feel God's pleasure." I begin to feel God's pleasure as I work my body to physical exhaustion. I am surprised by how much extra my body still has to give.

I wish all clergy could experience the means of Grace that physical exercise has been for me. But I know that won't happen. I have learned to be less evangelical about my exercise program, knowing that only a few will actually take the plunge. I recall a fellow Lutheran pastor ten years my junior who attended one of my stress workshops. He was thirty pounds overweight and was involved in no physical regimen at all except for an occasional golf game. Tom liked me and he also liked to talk. I invited him to join me for a late afternoon run. As we circled the convent once he had to stop to rest as I went around again. He joined me for half the cycle and had to drop off again. I both intrigued and puzzled him with my stamina and endurance. By the end of the run I felt I had hooked him.

That was fifteen years ago. Since then Tom has peeled down to 140 pounds and run marathons and triathalons. I am now the one who is amazed at his stamina and endurance.

For many of you, exercise is pure work and agony. You do it because you know it is good for you. Yet if you had your druthers you would much rather be a couch potato. My wish for you is that you might reach a level of physical conditioning that will enable you to experience some of the exhilarating benefits of a hard physical workout. Yes, there is such a thing as a runner's high. At certain levels of fatigue the brain releases endorphins into the blood stream. These chemicals are the body's own pain relievers and serve to elevate the runner's feelings. When the "high" hits, you get a second wind and you feel you could run forever. This same sense of euphoria can come to walkers, swimmers, and cyclists, but it comes only occasionally, and then only after you have been working at it for an hour or more.

Beyond the conditioning and the weight control, vigorous exercise gives one an emotional and spiritual lift. I am not the only one who writes sermons and presentations while on a run. If I have a sermon to prepare, after I have done some basic research on a biblical text I put on my running shoes and start running. After an hour of pumping up hills and sweating it out, the sermon outline is usually fairly clear. I have lots of life examples that relate to the text. I don't know why my creativity is enhanced so much during a run, but it is. Some claim that vigorous exercise pumps more blood through your brain. A colleague, Tom Tupper, always keeps a notepad hanging on a clipboard on his porch so he can write down ideas that have occurred to him on his run. The notepad looks pretty ratty by now because he writes things down when his hands and arms are dripping with sweat.

Emotionally, vigorous exercise tends to give us a boost. It tends to elevate our mood and give us protection against depression. A good workout tends to distract our minds from troubles and also serves as a healthy release for anger and anxiety. I would describe myself as a fairly anxious person most of the time. What running or swimming does for me is give me an hour of anxious-free space from which to view my life. That perspective often turns my anxiety around and helps me be more joyful and grateful. There is the additional benefit of heightened self-esteem that comes from having a fitter body and a feeling of ease with our general state of health.

Weight control is another clear benefit of vigorous exercise. Walking or running burns calories—that's 600 calories if you slow jog six miles in an hour. Burning 600 calories will help significantly with weight loss or maintenance. Yet the biggest boost for the dieter is the fact that exercising actually suppresses hunger. When I sit around being very sedentary, I usually have a voracious appetite. When I run, swim, or walk for an hour my hunger actually dissipates. Many dieters find they can peel off pounds fast by skipping lunch and going for a workout. The heavier the workout, the less they feel the hunger. Hunger usually abates for several hours after a vigorous workout.

The Limits of Our Mind

There was a time when we thought it was humanly impossible for a person to run a four-minute mile! Yet the year Roger Banister broke the four-minute mile, two other people also accomplished the same feat. Today, runners are not even considered for Olympic competition unless they can run a four-minute mile.

A similar experience happened to me three years ago when my colleague here at The Alban Institute, Loren Mead, told me he had entered and completed the Bay Bridge Swim held each year at the Chesapeake Bay Bridge in Annapolis, Maryland. The race is 4.4 miles through tidal waters. Loren is six years older than I am, and the fact that he was able to swim 4.4 miles in open water made me think it was possible for me too. In 1988 we both entered, but because there was a strong tide that year we both got disqualified when the tide pushed us outside the spans of the bridge. In 1989 we both completed the race, I in 3 hours 39 minutes and Loren in 3 hours 41 minutes. This past year, Loren completed the race in 2 hours 55 minutes and I in 3 hours 35 minutes. Loren has presented me with another challenge: to trim 40 minutes off my time in that race in order to keep up with him! Regardless of who wins the race, completing the swim is the target. Had it not been for Loren, I would never have tried. My mind had put a limitation on my body's ability to complete that feat.

If you see all this physical activity as being totally outside the realm of possibility for you, ask yourself whether you have allowed your body to become captive to your mind. If you tell yourself you can't do something, then indeed you can't. Yet hidden inside of you is a healthier, trimmer, physically fit person you might not even recognize. Can you even for a moment get in touch with the spiritual, emotional, and physical high it would be for you to have this healthier you emerge from within? I'm not saying it will be easy. But if you can at least get started, you may be surprised at the level of physical fitness that is possible for you.

You've heard about late bloomers, those people who have not exercised a lick until their late fifties and sixties. Some of these people get in such good condition they begin to enter marathons and swim meets. What they have discovered is that even in advanced age the body actually develops new muscles through vigorous exercise. They are able to reach a level of physical conditioning far beyond what they could have accomplished twenty years earlier.

In a study conducted at Harvard Medical School, frail, institutionalized volunteers, male and female, between eighty-six and ninety-six years old began doing leg lifts on a weight bench for forty-five minutes per session, three times a week, over a period of eight weeks. At the conclusion of the study, measurements of strength more than doubled on the average; leg muscle size increased as much as 13.5 percent; and walking speed increased by nearly fifty percent. Two participants who previously needed canes quit using them altogether, and another subject who couldn't get out of a chair without leaning on the arms became able to do so. The authors of the study noted that the participants' responsiveness was "remarkable in light of their very advanced age, extremely sedentary habits, multiple chronic diseases and functional disabilities, and nutritional inadequacies."[3]

Take a minute now and close your eyes for a visualization exercise. After some quiet deep breathing, see if you can visualize within you a healthier, trimmer, more physically fit person. Try to enter into how it would feel being that healthier you. Try to picture what you would look like. Picture yourself walking down your street. Note the surprise you see in other people's faces as they meet this new you. Hear yourself talking to them, answering their questions about how you were able to accomplish your physical fitness. Get a sense of your level of self-esteem. Also get in touch with the increased energy you would have available to you. Do not let your sense of failure with other attempts to become healthier sidetrack this visualization. Simply stay with the

sounds, feelings, and images that occur to you as you become the
healthier person who waits inside of you.

Choosing the Right Exercise

Exercise can serve many purposes. It can enhance skills, improve flexibility, build muscle strength and tone, relieve tension, help in weight loss
and maintenance, and improve the body's general physiological condition, especially the ease with which the heart can supply oxygen to body
tissues. Particular types of exercise may serve some of these functions,
but not others. For example, bowling and golf can help you become
more skillful at the game, strengthen certain muscles, and expend energy
(calories), but they rarely involve enough continuous activity to condition your cardiovascular system.

Isometric exercises, such as weight-lifting, water-skiing and arm-
wrestling and which clamp down on muscles, will promote strong
muscles but are useless—in fact, countereffective—as cardiovascular
conditioners and may actually be harmful to persons with heart disease.
On the other hand, brisk walking may do little for your athletic skills or
muscle strength, but it can be highly beneficial to your heart and figure.

Most people start exercising because they want to look better and
feel better. Often, however, the chosen activity spurs a change or ex-
pansion of goals. For example, those who take up tennis to reduce
tension or flab may find themselves huffing and puffing on the court.
Realizing that they are "out of condition," they may start running or
cycling to improve their body's ability to deliver oxygen to their
muscles.

In choosing an exercise, it's important to know what you hope to get
out of it and whether that choice will help you achieve your goals. Having a clear objective will help you visualize your hoped-for outcome.
This in turn will assist you in moving through those inevitable periods of
discouragement when you find it hard to stick to your regimen. The
clearer you can be about what you hope to get out of your exercise program, the more able you will be to work through either your psychic or
your physical barriers.

Any kind of motion involves the expenditure of calories, and the
more you move, the more calories you burn. The heavier you are to start

with, the more calories it takes to move yourself a given distance. In addition, moderate exercise improves the accuracy of your body's appetite control mechanism and more frequently decreases rather than increases appetite.

You don't have to sweat or exercise strenuously to use energy. In fact, walking a mile burns the same number of calories as running a mile. The difference, as far as calories are concerned, is that running a mile is faster and you may then have time to run a second mile and use up twice as many calories.

Some activities are intense energy guzzlers, using eight or more times the amount of calories your body burns at rest. These activities include running more than 5.5 miles an hour, cycling thirteen or more miles an hour, playing squash and handball, and skipping rope. But you can burn as many calories playing ping-pong or volleyball for an hour as you would running for half an hour.

To maximize the conditioning effect (fitness or endurance) of exercise, the activity should use the large muscles in a rhythmic, repetitive, continuous motion—so called isotonic exercises. A cardiovascular conditioning exercise must also be aerobic, that is, it promotes the use of oxygen and can be sustained for at least two minutes at a time without your getting out of breath. To condition the cardiovascular system, the exercise should be performed at least three times a week for twenty minutes at a time, during which the heart rate is within the individual's target zone, which is seventy to eighty-five percent of the maximum rate your heart can achieve. The maximum heart rate (or pulse rate) counted as beats per minute can be estimated for the average healthy adult as 220 minus your age. Take seventy to eighty-five percent of that number and you will have your target pulse rate.

Your choice of an exercise will depend on the time you have available, your age, health status and present physical condition, the cost and convenience of certain facilities, and your body's capabilities. There is no best exercise for everyone. You are more likely to stick with an exercise that you enjoy, but you should give a new activity a trial of a month or two before deciding you don't like it.

CHAPTER 17

Monitoring Our Intake

For the most part, we North Americans are over-fed and malnourished. Unhealthy eating patterns afflict our population across socioeconomic boundaries. With such abundance and variety of food available to us, it's a continual test not to over-consume. The foods that twang our taste buds the most are also the ones that are killing us. Those who have learned to eat wisely have trained their palate to enjoy more healthful foods.

The first time I ever tasted Scotch whiskey I thought it was the most vile thing I had ever put in my mouth. I could not imagine how anyone could like the taste of Scotch. But I watched my friends drink Scotch and soda, and occasionally I gave it a try. It still didn't taste very good. Then something changed in my life. For whatever reasons, I began to need alcohol in my system on a daily basis. I began to shun the sweeter drinks, and Scotch and water began to have more appeal. At the height of my burnout and depression just before my divorce, I was consuming a tumbler of Scotch and water every night. Later when my life began to get straightened out through some therapy and a change of jobs, I really didn't need the alcohol in my system anymore. Yet I was hooked on the taste of Scotch and water. I could not find a drink that pleased my palate more. To this day, even though I no longer consume any hard alcohol, the occasional sip of Scotch and water has a good aroma to it.

That experience taught me something important: if I could train myself to like Scotch, I could train myself to enjoy just about anything. Since then I have been training myself to enjoy more than anything else the food that is good for me. I have also become aware of how nauseating I now find some foods that I used to enjoy. Foods rich in butter and cream may taste good on the first bite, but something tells me this is not good for me, and suddenly they don't taste so good anymore. Last winter on the way home from a trip, my wife Carole and I stopped in at a restaurant for dinner. She ordered a steak. On the way out of the restaurant she confided that she was never going to do that again. She enjoyed her steak, but couldn't tolerate the look I had on my face as I watched her eat it. It was purely unconscious on my part, but in retrospect I did think the steak looked awfully greasy.

Poor eating patterns compound the difficulties related to excessive stress and burnout. When our bodies are assaulted by battering rams of emotional turmoil all day, and then we assault them even more with caffeine, sugar, salt, fat, alcohol, and refined flour, it's like a one-two punch. We could alleviate much of the stress and burnout in our lives simply by eating regular, balanced meals at appropriate times during the day.

Limiting Certain Foods

We would do ourselves a great favor if cut down our consumption of four basic foods: sugar, salt, white flour, and saturated fat.

Sugar is empty calories. Sugar beets or sugar cane are healthy foods if we consume them directly. But when the sugar is refined out of these plants, all the fiber and other nutritional substances are eliminated. All that's left are empty calories that tend to throw our metabolism off balance. Whenever we consume large amounts of sugar, our pancreas must work overtime to create enough insulin to cope with it. Over-consumption of sugar is also the number one contributor to obesity, and sugar diabetes strikes overweight people three times more frequently than those who maintain their recommended weight.

Nothing makes our taste buds come alive quite like sugar. We demand that it be in most of our favorite foods. You have to look long and hard to find a breakfast cereal that does not have sugar as its second or third ingredient. So, along with some whole grains that are good for you, usually you're getting a large amount of sugar in your morning cereal. Sugar is also the second ingredient in most cakes, cookies, pies, ice creams, and other desserts. Sugar is the third ingredient in ketchup. We would not like our tomato soup or our stewed tomatoes without sugar in them. A ten-ounce can of Pepsi contains ten teaspoons of sugar. If you don't believe this, allow a Pepsi to stay out overnight. Take a sip when it is at room temperature without the carbonation. Generally, the more sugar a manufacturer puts in a product, the more we like it.

Salt is the next ingredient we like on our tongue. It's hard to imagine a junk food without salt (potato chips, corn chips, pretzels, crackers, etc.) Yet salt is the chief cause of some people's hypertension (high blood pressure). If it isn't stress that's pushing your blood pressure up, it's probably the salt. One out of every two people in North America is sodium sensitive, which means that their blood pressure is especially sensitive to salt intake. If you are a white male age thirty-five with a blood pressure of 150/100, it is estimated that your life will be shortened by twenty-eight years if you don't bring your blood pressure down. At age forty-five, the decrease in life expectancy with that level of blood pressure is 11.5 years. At age sixty-five, the decrease in life expectancy is six years. While women tolerate high blood pressure better than men, and it may take higher pressure to hurt women, the threat is still a serious one for them.

Hypertension seems to afflict Afro-American males even more seriously than white males. It is estimated that one in every three black Americans over eighteen has high blood pressure. One contributor to hypertension may be the stress of being black and male in our culture, but it may also be true that blacks are more sodium sensitive than whites.

The body does require some salt in order to function well. We each need about 200 milligrams, or about one-eighth of a teaspoon, of salt a day. Fill the tip of your little finger with salt, and that's all the salt you need in a day, yet each of us consumes about ten times that amount.

White flour, that white powdery stuff that shows up in most of our baked goods, is considered a key contributor to diseases of the digestive tract. Approximately 60,000 people in the United States die of colon cancer each year. Deaths from this disease could be diminished considerably if we would consume far more fiber-rich foods than white flour. Do you re-member how we used to make glue in first grade? You got it. We sim-ply mixed flour and water to make a sticky, pasty substance that worked like any good glue. Eating products made with white flour is like eating glue. When we put large amounts of that stuff into our bodies, our digestive tract has difficulty processing it through the system. It gets stuck in there and begins to decay.

Do not be fooled by the term "enriched flour." It should be called "impoverished flour" because it's the same white powder, only it's been sprayed with several vitamins you don't need. It's the bran and the wheat germ that you need, and that's been taken out in processing the flour.

The label "Whole Wheat Bread" is also deceptive. Bakeries can call bread whole wheat if the third ingredient is whole wheat. Read the label: ninety-five percent of the bread in your grocery has as its first ingredient "enriched flour." The next ingredient is water. By volume you are getting very little actual whole wheat. In addition, most of our noodles, pastas, cakes, cookies, and pies are also made from this impoverished white flour.

The reason so much white flour is used in this country is because it keeps forever (almost). Whole wheat products spoil rather rapidly. Besides, stores can then sell wheat germ and bran separately.

To keep tasty, nutritious bread in our house we order it through the mail. A bakery that makes good whole wheat products can ship out a dozen loaves that will arrive at your home via UPS in two days. Pop those into your freezer, and you'll have quality bread on hand.[1]

Eliminating the sugar, salt, white flour, and saturated fats from your diet would definitely change your food intake. What about that donut in the morning? Take away the four ingredients above and all you're left with is the hole. But substituting fruit for those donuts and Danish each morning would contribute greatly to your health.

Restricting Fat Intake

A colleague recently peeled off twenty pounds of extra weight simply by cutting down on his consumption of fat. He didn't cut down the volume of food he was eating; he simply restricted his diet to low-fat foods. Nutritionists and the American Heart Association recommend that fat not exceed thirty percent of the total calories we consume. Statistics indicate, however, that the average American diet consists of forty-two percent or more of fat. The Pritikin Diet recommends that fat equal no more than ten percent of one's normal intake.

Nathan Pritikin himself gives testimony to the fact that simply changing one's diet can effectively reverse arteriosclerosis (the building up of fatty deposits in the arteries restricting blood flow and increasing the possibility of heart attack). Pritikin was told that he had severe arteriosclerosis and would need bypass surgery. He decided to try another route, namely, altering his diet. He cut his fat consumption down to less than ten percent of his diet. When Nathan Pritikin died two years ago, an autopsy revealed that his arteries were clean as a whistle. Norman Cousins, in his book *The Healing Heart*, details how he followed a similar course to avoid bypass surgery.[2] He too recently died, but not until after living a long active life far beyond the expectations of his doctors.

A recent study cited in the *Journal of the American Medical Association* stressed that dietary changes alone should be sufficient to lower moderate levels of cholesterol and that achieving these lower levels may help reverse heart disease. One hundred sixty-two men who had had heart bypass surgery were divided into two groups. The first group was given a combination of two cholesterol-lowering drugs and a strict low-fat, low-cholesterol diet. The other "control" group took placebos and was allowed to eat a higher fat diet. The study found that:

– Cholesterol levels declined an average of 26 percent in the treated men compared to 4 percent in the control group.

– Heart disease progressed in 38 percent of the treated men compared to 61 percent of the control group men.

– Fatty deposits shrank in 16.2 percent of the treated men compared to 2.4 percent in the control group men.

The drugs used in the study to lower cholesterol were colestipol and niacin, each of which have only minor side effects. I have used the vitamin niacin in combination with a daily intake of oat bran, plus a reduction of fat intake, to bring my cholesterol level below the recommended 180 milligrams per deciliter of blood. Physicians used to recommend that cholesterol levels of 240 milligrams per deciliter were acceptable. Recently, on the basis of more research on heart disease, doctors are recommending that the number be 200 or less, preferably below 180.[3]

Cutting down on the consumption of red meat helps a lot in lowering the fat in our diets. Countries where red meat is rarely consumed have one quarter the incidence of heart disease of countries where beef and lamb are eaten regularly.

Rather than having red meat once a day, try having it only one or two times a week. Use skinless chicken and fish as substitutes.

If you have heart disease in your family tree, as I do, it's encouraging to know that there are some specific things to do to keep ourselves from succumbing to that disease. I see diet and exercise as being like two pit bulls standing guard out front to protect me from the heart marauder!

Choosing a Weight-Loss Program

If you are among the sixty-two million Americans who are seriously overweight and want to do something about taking off the pounds, you have a variety of choices. This is assuming you have tried on your own to take off the weight and find you are unable to sustain your self-prescribed disciplines. Each of the various weight-loss programs have some liabilities, so you may need help in choosing well. The $33-billion-a-year weight loss industry feeds into our society's "quick fix" mentality, and the problems go beyond any one company.

All diet programs have the same objective—to help you lose weight —but they vary in their approach. If you buy over-the-counter products such as Slim Fast and Ultra Slim Fast, for example, you are essentially prescribing the plan yourself. The "real food" diets, like Weight Watchers and Jenny Craig, try to help you slim down without special shakes or formulas. And the very low calorie programs—HMR, Medifast, and Optifast—are medically supervised and usually accept only those who are at least twenty-eight percent over their ideal weight. Even within these major categories, however, there is considerable variation, and some people may fare better with one plan than another.

A fantastic exchange of energy occurs every time we put solid food into our bodies. The body is never static. It's like a river, ever changing. Over a twelve-month period, ninety-eight percent of our body has been refurbished with new cells. Our skin changes itself once every thirty days. Our liver is made over completely every six weeks. Even our brain, in terms of the carbon and hydrogen molecules, renews itself every twelve months. Many of us test the genius of this recreative process when we feed our bodies junk instead of good foods. I hope we can begin to appreciate our bodies for the magnificent organisms they are, especially when we're reaching for that next gin and tonic or donut. We'll not only be adding years to our life, but during those extra years we'll feel better than we ever imagined.

CHAPTER 18

The Psychotherapy Tune-Up

There are times in our ministries when the cynicism, the disillusionment, and the self-depreciation are so deeply entrenched that we need some professional help to find our way out of the quagmire. Cynicism, a hallmark of burnout, does not come upon us suddenly. It brews for a long time. Usually, we're totally out of touch with how cynicism has discolored our life. Once discovered—usually because someone who cares about us points it out—cynicism is not easily overcome. Therapy is one strategy many have used to make their way back to vitality and optimism.

Being in therapy is like having someone in your corner to confer with after each round in the ring. When you try to say "No" to some demand and get beaten severely by either anger or a guilt trip, you have somewhere to go to lick your wounds and develop a strategy for how you will handle that person or situation in the next round. This is the kind of support we need to make the radical changes necessary for our own survival, health, and wholeness.

The roots of our burnout are almost always hidden from us. There are some internal messages or self-perceptions that keep us on a treadmill that leads to our own destruction. Uncovering these hidden drives, these distorted self-images, usually requires the aid of an objective outsider. Because these inner forces are rooted deep in the unconscious, it may take more than one conversation to surface them and deal with them. It will take some digging and processing over an extended period of time. I recommend staying in therapy for a minimum of six months before concluding that you have dealt with the roots of your burnout.

Self-depreciation is also a symptom of burnout. Burnout victims generally blame themselves for the trouble they are in. They often fail to see that they are victims of systems that have burned others out before them. Therapy can be an important way to gain distance and perspective on your work. It can help you see that you are taking on much more of the blame for your malaise than you deserve.

Therapy as Professional Development

Therapy, when it works well, leads to greater health and wholeness. This, in turn, helps us become more effective pastors. The healthier we are, the greater will be our ability to invite others into a healthier state. In this sense, therapy should be considered part of our professional development.

To become a Jungian analyst one needs to spend six years in personal analysis. The same is true for other schools of psychoanalysis. These would-be therapists are required to log a certain number of hours of therapy themselves because that experience really gives them the foundation they need to be good people helpers. Yet we as clergy have no such requirement before offering pastoral counseling to others. We are bound to make better pastoral counselors if at some point we ourselves have been recipients of therapy. How is it that we feel free to assist others in exploring the internal chaos of their lives when we ourselves have never faced our own?

Health versus Sickness Model

If we look at therapy from the viewpoint of the medical model, we will not engage in this helpful art unless we really consider ourselves to be sick. The medical model says you must have an acute pathology to get treatment. You need to be experiencing some severe neurosis or psychosis before you look for a therapist. But the health model says that we can move from health to greater health. We can be quite functional, yet be held back from enjoying life by some addiction or childhood issue. Entering therapy may be the way we reach our full potential as a human beings. As such, therapy can legitimately be considered continuing education or professional development. In the ordained ministry, anything that helps us become more free and whole will increase our professional competence.

Therapy for Men

More women than men seek therapy because, according to Dr. Jeffrey Cohen, Ph.D., our society has conditioned women to talk about their problems and accept advice from others. Men, in contrast, have been conditioned to be strong, silent types who can take care of themselves. Even though this has changed in the last ten years, men still lag behind women in seeking therapy as a helpful alternative. Ten years ago, about thirty percent of all people in therapy were men. Today the number is closer to forty-five percent.

One problem with therapy for men is this: Many therapists treat men and women the same when they should be treated differently. The main differences I see between men and women in therapy are:

—Men still resist committing themselves to the therapeutic process. A man often comes to therapy because of a crisis—his wife has threatened to leave him or his boss has threatened to fire him or he has problems with his kids.

—Men are focused on symptom resolution. They are not willing to stay in therapy as long as women are.

—Men are extremely sensitive to disapproval. They can easily become reticent or disengaged, particularly if the therapist becomes confrontational.

Choosing a Therapist

As clergy differ, so do therapists. It is worth the time and energy to select one carefully before committing yourself to internal work. Ask your friends and colleagues which therapists they recommend and why. A few names will be repeated enough to give you confidence in their skill, approach, and trustworthiness. Make an exploratory visit to each person to determine if the two of you can work effectively together.

The most important criteria for choosing a therapist is this: you need to like each other. Early in his career, Carl Rogers conducted research on the various schools of psychology to determine if one approach was better than others. He compared Freudians, Jungians, Adlerians, and

Eriksonians, and, in the end, discovered that there was no one school of psychology that stood out above all the others. Instead, he found that when the therapist liked the client, the client tended to get well, regardless of the orientation of the therapist. Conversely, when the therapist did not like the client, little of significance happened, regardless of the school of thought of the therapist. This study has enormous implication for us as clergy. We need to recognize that there are limits to how helpful we can be to people we dislike. Therapy may help us with our hangups with certain people, but don't make the mistake of thinking that a therapist can help you when you don't believe that he or she likes you.

Beyond the "liking" issue, be sure to test the therapist's disposition and beliefs about matters of theology and faith. S/he needs to respect that this is an integral part of you and that at some point s/he may need to help you struggle with these issues. The choice of a male therapist versus a female therapist may be determined by the issues you feel you want to address. For example, if you're a man, seeing a woman therapist may help you in dealing with issues of sexuality or your relationship with your mother or your difficulties with female coworkers.

Financing Therapy

Most church health or pension programs will pay part of the cost of therapy. Check it out, especially noting the conditions under which they will pay. Unfortunately, many church health plans still work on the medical model; they will subsidize treatment if you can be considered "emotionally ill." If this describes your health plan, check with your therapist to see if s/he feels your case would qualify for insurance subsidy. My therapist's label for me did the trick with my pension plan. I never asked how he classified me. I needed help and was less interested in the label.

Some judicatories have found ways to subsidize therapy while safeguarding their clergy's anonymity. These systems are to be commended. Still, many church systems make no provisions for the professional care of their clergy, even if they burn out. This might be excusable if these denominations had offered clergy training in survival skills while in parish ministry. But in the absence of such training, the lack of therapeutic support for clergy who burn out seems downright exploitive. It boils down to poor management when those in authority don't have a game plan for how they are going to keep their best clergy functioning well when they run into emotional upheaval or difficulty.

Therapy is not inexpensive. You may feel you can't afford it on your salary. On the other hand, therapy may be the kind of assistance you can't afford to bypass. If it can reverse the cycle of burnout in your life and return you to health and vitality, it is help you can't afford to miss. If, however, there is absolutely no financial support for therapy within your denomination, you should feel justified in jumping up and down at appropriate gatherings and demanding such support. The caveat is to do this well in advance of the time when you need therapy desperately. When your backside is scraping bottom, you won't have either the energy or the confidence to take on your middle judicatory.

Also, be sure to locate a therapist well in advance of your needing one badly. When you are burned out and depressed, one of the last things you want to do is to interview a bunch of therapists. A good therapist should be part of the support network all clergy develop as they begin ministry in a new location.

CHAPTER 19

Getting Control of Our Time

The great paradox regarding time is that no one seems to have enough of it, yet each of us has all there is.

Alex MacKenzie, in a ten-year study of time utilization, found a significant relationship between how managers use their time and their level of stress.[1] Certain time wasting activities produced particularly high stress. MacKenzie identified seven danger signals of stress; if we experience three or four of these, our stress level is probably high, and poor time management may be the cause:

1. The belief that we are indispensable.
2. No time for important tasks. Crisis consistently robs us of time for top priorities.
3. Attempting too much. We constantly underestimate the time and effort it will take to complete tasks. An inability to say "no" is part of this. We think we can do it all.
4. Constant unrelenting pressure. We always feel we're behind and won't be able to get on top of our job.
5. Habitual long hours.
6. Guilt about leaving work early.
7. Taking worry home with us. We are physically at home, but our minds are back on the job. Preoccupying worries of the day take precedence over family and personal activities.

MacKenzie concluded that longer hours do not necessarily mean greater productivity. In fact, more often than not, the reverse is true. Past a certain point, productivity declines rapidly. We need to learn the limits of our stress and schedule our work within those limits.

In any task a certain amount of stress is needed to get us moving and keep us on our creative edge. Productivity increases with stress until a certain critical point is reached. Beyond that critical point, productivity drops rapidly.

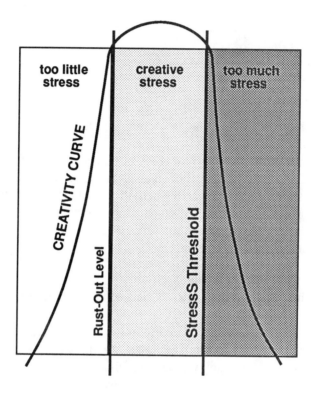

The relationship between stress and time management is clear. At certain levels, stress becomes a counter-productive time waster.

Several times now, I have said that I believe clergy should try to complete their professional work in fifty hours per week or less. Otherwise we will probably sacrifice our physical health (through lack of time for rest, exercise, and healthy eating habits), our family (through lack of quality time with them), or our spiritual life (through lack of time for reflection, prayer, study, and other spiritual disciplines). Both minister and parish lose when one or more of these aspects of life is diminished.

It is our responsibility to learn to complete all the important tasks of our calling in that timeframe. Giving our best in fifty hours and managing our time well is the most that can be expected of us. Each of us probably manages most of our time well, but we may have areas in which we are wasting time because of issues we refuse to confront. Time is a non-expandable commodity. We cannot manage time better. Time manages itself quite well—it just keeps going. We must learn to manage *ourselves* better.

Each of us finds time for the most important things in life. If the things that now receive our attention and time aren't important to us, why are we spending time on them? A good way to assess whether we are spending time on the most important areas of our jobs and our personal lives is to do a time study. It requires discipline to record and analyze your use of time. Pick a two-week period when you can record your time in either thirty- or sixty-minute blocks. There are 168 hours in a week. Account for each of those hours. First, break the time down into three categories—professional time, family time, and personal time—and put your activities into the appropriate section. Make sure each activity you record can be listed legitimately in one category. If it doesn't fit, make a new category.

In the Douglass/McNally study,[2] clergy were asked to record how they divided their 168 hours in one week. The following is the average for all seventeen clergy:

	Hours	Percent
Ministry	56	33.3%
Personal Life	41	24.4%
Rest at Night	56	33.3%
Unaccounted-for Time	15	9.0%
Total Life	168	100.0%

The following shows how the clergy divided their fifty-six hours at work—and how they would have preferred to spend those hours.

	Preferred Piority	Actual Priority	Actual % of fime spent
Preacher	1	2	20%
Pastor	2	3	18%
Theologian	3	4	14%
Marketer	4	6	4%
Administrator	5	1	33%
Traveler	6	5	11%

Now you can judge. Are you spending the amount of you want on personal time, family time, professional time? What is your ideal division between these three? How does it differ from the actual? What do you want to change? Who will you need to support you in this effort?

Next, analyze the way you spend time within these categories. What changes do you wish to make and how? Consider what support you will need for these changes.

What are the essential tasks in your professional life that need to be completed each week? List them in descending order of priority. If emergencies or personal crises arise and you have time to do only one thing on your list, what would that one thing be? What would be next after that, etc.? This listing puts your weekly activities in perspective.

None of the clergy in the Douglass/McNally study reported having well-clarified objectives for their ministry. Neither ministers nor their churches did a good job in this respect. Yet effective time management requires our working toward identifiable and measurable goals.

Goal-setting may be the roughest challenge for clergy in gaining role clarity with the parish. Both the pastor and the parish must agree on the activities that should receive priority pastoral time.

Role Clarity

Getting a clear sense of your weekly priorities is only half the battle. Everyone else in the parish has an idea of how you ought to spend your time, too. Role negotiation is tough and never-ending, but essential if your time is to be managed well. Start with your official board. You will need their support if you are to stick with a time management plan. Share your time study with them. Lay people often have no idea how a pastor spends his/her time; they have difficulty understanding where sixty to eighty hours per week could be spent. They need to know where your time goes if they are to support you in limiting your work week to fifty hours or less. They will have to agree on what the priorities of your work should be, and they must decide how responsibilities you will not be able to handle are to be managed.

One important principle to remember in negotiating time with your lay board: always build in time to manage emergencies and crises, ministry events, and other occasional pastoral duties. What percentage of your time is to be spent on funerals, weddings, serious illness, or problems with parishioners? Many clergy estimate that approximately twenty percent of their time is spent on nonscheduled events. This means that your work plan should reserve ten hours for emergencies.

There will probably be considerable discussion by your board on your time priorities. This is important. Then, when parishioners complain about things you have not done for them, you will have your board's backing on your time priorities.

Clergy Time Wasters

The top five time wasters identified by clergy in the Douglass/McNally study were:

1. Interruptions (telephone calls, drop-in visitors, distractions)
2. Tasks left unfinished (jumping from one thing to another)

3. Routine tasks involving too much trivia
4. Attempts to do too much at once (unrealistic time estimates)
5. Personal disorganization (i.e., cluttered desk and office).

Douglass and McNally noticed a disparity between clergy's knowing what to do and actually doing it. For instance:

— Ministers indicated that they could find many ways to save time, yet few had done so.
— Most ministers said they could control their schedules, yet lack of workable schedules was a major problem.
— Most ministers reported that they usually worked on the basis of priorities, but observation indicated they frequently did not.
— Most ministers agreed that it is necessary to write out objectives, but few did.
— All ministers agreed that planning is an important part of their ministry, but none spent as much time planning as they felt they should.
— Most ministers reported that they did not have enough time for new member recruitment, yet office breaks took as much time as the entire marketer role.

Work to a Plan

The key to resolving such discrepancies is the development of the discipline of working to a plan. This is one way to gain the full value of time. Without such a plan, one drifts from task to task, finishing few and not really tackling the most important.

Because rest and relaxation are vital to our effectiveness, we need to build leisure time into our daily and weekly schedule. Central to this is taking time at the beginning of the week to work out goals and objectives. Each day should begin with time for planning the tasks that are to be accomplished and their deadlines. Use a list or cards to outline your daily activities. Stick with your plan except for emergencies.

Here are some other ways to save time:

— Never handle a piece of paper more than once. For instance, don't open and read your mail until you are ready to answer it.

— Develop a scheme for managing telephone calls. They can seriously interrupt work flow, yet they are a major way for people to be in touch with you.

— Get an answering service if you don't have one.

There are several good resources available for digging deeper into time management. I highly recommend a book by my Alban Institute colleague Speed B. Leas, *Time Management: A Working Guide for Church Leaders*.[3] I've also heard glowing reports about the time management seminars sponsored by World Vision International. Participants have said that these folks have put together a superb two-day course that is intensive, fun, yet deeply spiritual.[4]

So let's not waste another minute! Now's the time to get control of your time.

CHAPTER 20

The Value of
Assertiveness Training

Good self-care habits clearly involve being able to assert our needs in the face of the demands of others. Without this ability, we become victims of every situation. As Rollo May points out so dramatically in his book *Power and Innocence*,[1] without the ability to assert ourselves we will have difficulty living with integrity and self-respect. Sacrificing our rights usually trains others to mistreat us. By standing up for our rights, we show we respect ourselves and thus win the respect of others.

Assertiveness training has been an enormously helpful tool in assisting people gain control of their lives. As such, it is a most helpful tool for persons experiencing burnout. Most clergy are deeply caring persons who constantly have their antennae up, scanning the horizon for the pain and suffering of parishioners and non-members alike. This is a key strength that needs to be protected, but we also need to acknowledge that an overuse of strengths can become a weakness. An overuse of our ability to care, to be sensitive and perceptive, and to notice the pain of others can result in our becoming strung out and emotionally depleted. We become easy prey for people who either consciously or unconsciously exploit the caring feelings of others to gain attention, power, or affection. In the long run, we become less effective ministers.

Of course, for some clergy a lack of assertiveness is a life-long pattern. They grew up denying their own needs. A low self-image may have contributed to this pattern or perhaps they were taught by parents that they did not deserve to have their personal needs fulfilled. Some may have been taught that it was un-Christian to take their own needs seriously. Many of us learned the cute little Sunday School lesson which said that you could experience J-O-Y by putting Jesus first, Others second, Yourself last. That's a perfect prescription for becoming unassertive and self-deprecating.

Central to assertiveness training is knowing and comprehending at various levels the distinction between:

Passive/Non-Assertive   Assertive   Aggressive
Behavior   Behavior   Behavior

The Passive, Non-Assertive Person:

— denies self,
— is usually inhibited, hurt, and anxious,
— continually defers to others in making choices for his/her life, and
— is usually ineffective as a person and/or as a professional.

The Aggressive Person:

— enhances the self at the expense of others,
— tends to depreciate others,
— tries to decide matters for others, and
— normally achieves desired goals, but hurts others in the process.

The Assertive Person:

– is self-enhancing,
– expresses positive feeling about self,
– chooses for self and accepts consequences, and
– usually achieves desired goals, yet not at the expense of others.

Many of us believe that an assertive person is a hostile, aggressive person. We need to change that notion if we are to be effectively assertive. An assertive person is usually a deeply caring person who expresses many positive feelings towards others. Such a person usually can express clearly, firmly, and yet in a nonhostile manner who they are and what they need. As such they remain autonomous, joyous people.

Of the three alternatives–passive, aggressive, or assertive behavior– it's clear that assertive behavior is the most effective for healthful living and productive work. The aggressive person digs his/her own grave. Once people catch on that the aggressive person will run over them like a tank, they learn to either counteract such tactics or to avoid the person altogether. Before long, aggressive people find themselves alienated and isolated. On the other hand, the passive person remains the ineffectual non-entity in our midst. They are the doormats who get walked on, but rarely noticed. On the other hand, when dealing with the assertive person, you are always clear about their wants, needs, and feelings. You may not like what they claim for themselves or the way they feel, but at least it's out in the open. And you can come to trust that they will not run over you in order to get their needs met. They will expect you to be assertive about your needs, too, and when needs clash, negotiation becomes the pathway that leads to resolution.

All of this is well and good, you say, but many of us were never taught how to assert ourselves in a healthy way. To take charge of our lives now means overcoming generations of messages, many internalized, that tell us not to be assertive. Moving out of either passive or aggressive behavior requires some disciplined, counter-acting training. We need to believe firmly that availing ourselves of opportunities for assertiveness training will not only increase our personal satisfaction, but also enhance our professional effectiveness.

If you don't want to commit yourself to attending a seminar on the subject, at least buy the books *Your Perfect Right*[2] and *Stand Up, Speak Out, and Talk Back*[3] by Albert and Emmons and work through the exercises. To help assess your assertiveness, I have developed the Clergy Assertive Behavior Rating Scale. Take a minute now to answer the questions honestly.

CLERGY ASSERTIVE BEHAVIOR RATING SCALE

	Never	Some-times	Occa-sionally	Fre-quently	Always
1. When invited to dinner where food that I consider either unhealthy or undesirable for me is served, I am able to decline politely.	1	2	3	4	5
2. I can be myself around wealthy, well-educated, or prestigious parishioners.	1	2	3	4	5
3. When a friend of mine is driving the car faster than is comfortable for me, I express my discomfort.	1	2	3	4	5
4. When being interviewed by a search committee of a parish I'm interested in, I express my needs and opinions clearly.	1	2	3	4	5
5. When a parish committee moves in a direction I oppose and my point of view is unpopular, I nonetheless state my opinion clearly.	1	2	3	4	5
6. I regularly am physically demonstrative of my love and caring for friends and family.	1	2	3	4	5
7. When a parishioner accepts a role or responsibility, yet consistently does not fulfill it, I reveal my feelings of being let down.	1	2	3	4	5
8. When I am lonely and depressed I take it seriously and ask people to assist me through the tough period.	1	2	3	4	5

9. I maintain eye contact in conversation with others.   1   2   3   4   5

10. I am able to receive parishioners' compliments on my work
and ministry without embarrass-
ment or a sense of obligation.   1   2   3   4   5

11. When a restaurant serves me
food that differs from what I
expected, I ask that the error be
corrected.   1   2   3   4   5

12. When I have completed an act
of ministry well, I tell others
about my accomplishments.   1   2   3   4   5

13. I ask for direction and help
when I need it.   1   2   3   4   5

14. I express my anger to someone who leaks a shared confidence.   1   2   3   4   5

15. When a parishioner makes an
unreasonable demand on my time,
I am able gently but firmly to hold
my ground.   1   2   3   4   5

16. When a project has been
accepted by my parish, I have
little difficulty asking individuals with means to make a substantial financial contribution to
the effort.   1   2   3   4   5

17. When a parish volunteer is not
performing up to expectations and
complaints are being voiced, I will
usually ask that they either meet
the criteria for the role or give up
the volunteer role.   1   2   3   4   5

18. When my secretary types a
letter that does not meet my stand-
ards for excellence, I will ask
him/her to retype the letter.   1   2   3   4   5

19. When a colleague in ministry
does not follow through on a commitment to attend a meeting I will
find a way to inform that peer of
my disappointment.   1   2   3   4   5

20. When I attend a continuing
education event and the instructor
does not live up to stated expectations, I will assert my needs so
as to get what I need from the
event.   1   2   3   4   5

Total of numbers circled _____

Clergy Assertive Behavior Rating Scale

    1-45   You are generally non-confrontive.
           You have a tendency to let things slide.
           Your life is often directed and controlled by others.

    45-75 You are assertive about your needs.

If your score is below 45, you may desire further support and
training in assertiveness; others may still be writing much of the agenda
for your life.

75-100 You may have a tendency towards aggressive behavior.
Much depends on how you present yourself.

One of the skills needed in assertiveness training is the ability to distinguish between assertive and aggressive behavior. When does being adamant about needs oppress someone else? The following guidelines may help:

Intent—Is it your intention to hurt the other or merely stand your ground?

Effect—What was the long-range effect of your behavior? Did someone get hurt in the process?

Social/Cultural Context—Asserting oneself on the street is different from doing so at a dinner party. The context will help define what is aggressive and what is assertive behavior.

Practical Steps in Gaining More Control Over Your Life

Step I
Choose one situation where you have continually been less assertive than desirable. Pick a situation that is not overly threatening to begin with. You should be reasonably confident that you can prevail.

Step II
Privately, fantasize the scenario as it usually is played out. Then fantasize the scene with you being more assertive of your needs and wants. Rerun that fantasy several times.

Step III (Optional)
In an assertiveness training workshop we would have you role play that situation, followed by a feedback session, or we would film you on videotape so you could watch yourself being more assertive and decide what you wanted to change. Training seminars can be helpful to us all. Being assertive is something we can all learn to do better. Enroll in a class if you get the chance.

Step IV
Execute your plan with confidence. Watch carefully for any moves that sabotage you in the process. Hold your ground as best you can.

Step V
Talk the incident over with a colleague, friend, or family member, exploring where you did well and where you could have done better. Ask them to stand by you as you try to become more comfortable with assertive behavior.

CHAPTER 21

The Power of Laughter

Research has demonstrated powerful links between our emotions and our physical health. Just as negative emotions, including anger and depression, can negatively affect physical health, so also positive emotional experiences, especially mirth and laughter, can have a beneficial physical effect.

Laughter is a total body experience. When we laugh we are exercising most of the major physiological systems of the body—the cardiovascular, respiratory, muscular, immune, and endocrine systems. Studies indicate that laughter decreases the perception of pain, improves respiration, increases the activity of the so-called killer cells and other lymphocytes, thus enhancing the immune function, and even provides an aerobic workout.

Laughter's effect on the body is biphasic—it both stimulates and relaxes. At the moment the mind perceives humor (the punch line) and laughter begins, bodily systems are stimulated. Once the laughter is over, a period of relaxation begins. For example, the heart rate increases during laughter and drops below normal for a few seconds afterwards, as it does in aerobic exercise. The muscles that participate in the physical act of laughing get a workout while those that do not participate relax. The late author and lecturer Norman Cousins claims to have cured himself from a crippling and supposedly irreversible disease with laughter. In 1964, Cousins came down with a serious collagen illness, a disease of the connective tissue. Cousins had great difficulty moving his limbs, even to turn over in bed. His prognosis was not good: he was told that the connective tissue in the spine would eventually disintegrate and his chances of recovery were one in five hundred. The specialist who treated Cousins had never witnessed a recovery from this disease.

With consultative help from his doctor, Cousins checked out of the hospital and embarked on his own healing process. Two ingredients were vital to his remarkable pathway back to health: massive doses of Vitamin C and *laughter*. In the midst of much pain, Cousins began watching re-runs of "Candid Camera" and Marx Brothers, W.C. Fields, and Abbott and Costello films. He discovered that a ten-minute belly laugh had an anesthetic effect and gave him at least two hours of painfree sleep. When the pain-killing effect of the laughter wore off, he switched to another film, and not infrequently it led to another pain-free sleep. Cousins had discovered a physiological basis for the ancient theory that laughter is good medicine. His book *Anatomy of an Illness*[1] testifies to this phenomenon.

Just as Cousins did, each one of us can build more laughter into our lives. We can set aside times for mirth and fun with family and friends. This can range from an unplanned evening by the fireplace making popcorn to a barn raising. We need to provide occasions to be together with people we enjoy and who enjoy us. The important ingredients are time, hospitable space, and arriving reasonably rested and unhassled. The rest will take care of itself.

Twice in my life I have run a marathon (26.3 miles)—first at age forty-five and again at age forty-seven. The only reason I did it a second time was because the first time was so painful I thought I had done something wrong. The second time was as bad as the first. With each race, however, I built into the experience an evening "Attaboy Party." About two dozen of my friends showed up for food, drink, and fun to celebrate my completing the race. Even though my legs were so sore I could hardly walk, I had a great time. We laughed a lot and I could feel healing going on at several levels.

How can you build laughs into your everyday work? Laughing only with friends at special events may be too meager a laugh diet. We need to build into our work settings the kind of climate that encourages relaxation and laughter. The staff at The Alban Institute is good for at least a couple of hearty laughs a week. They make a lot of hassles worthwhile.

Malcolm L. Kushner, in a book entitled *The Light Touch: How to Use Humor For Business Success*, makes a case for humor in the corporate world. Managers who use humor well appear to have a much easier time climbing the corporate ladder. This does not mean becoming the corporate clown or learning how to tell jokes. Good humor begins with the ability to laugh at oneself and moves from there to being able to see the funny side of corporate life. Enjoying the humor of others is key to being seen as having a good sense of humor. Once we have been able to communicate through a remark or two that we have a sense of humor, people's trust in us escalates, and they seem far more ready to listen to what we have to say.[2]

The ability to laugh is part of being human. Everyone has a sense of humor. Unfortunately, a person's readiness to laugh may be stifled as responsibilities mount or during times of stress. Ironically, those are the times when we most need a good laugh.

Many cultures have traditions that take this need for laughter into account. A good example is the Irish wake, where laughter and joyful sharing are part of the mourning process. Unfortunately, most people leave laughter to chance and don't take full advantage of its healing potential. I would recommend a two-step process:

1. Take your humor profile. For a day or a week, look for the kinds of things you think are funny. Make a deliberate effort to find out what makes you laugh.

2. Start a humor collection. Humor is available in many forms—books, magazines, videotapes, toys. Stock up on the writing of your favorite humor columnist. Tape a stand-up comedy show. Buy a silly face mask—whatever strikes your fancy. Then, when you have a down day or are fighting stress, go to your humor collection for a quick lift. It sounds simple, and it is. But most people don't think to do it.

One of the reasons I've included some cartoons in this book is to try to lighten up what can be a serious subject.

I believe that God is able to laugh and cry at the same time. There is much going on in the world that must bring a tear to the eyes of God, yet at the same time much of what's going on must appear downright funny. Sometimes I feel God suppressing a giggle when I've been deeply embroiled in some petty thing that has gone wrong in my life, and then God trips me up with a gorgeous sunset or other beautiful sight. It's almost as though God gets a kick out of breaking me out of my despondency with beauty, surprise, and laughter.

Because we are told in Scripture that there is absolutely nothing that can separate us from the love of God, we of all people, baptized and believing folk, are entitled to take life less seriously and laugh a bit more. We would all be a lot healthier, more productive, and helpful to others, and life and ministry would be a lot more fun.

If we both believe and experience God as not only a God of great love and compassion, but one with a sense of humor as well, we might free ourselves to do more laughing as we go about God's work. How about it? Did I ever tell you the one about the couple that...?

"Good news, Reverend. The board has voted to pray for your recovery . . .
the vote was 5 to 4."

CHAPTER 22

Monitoring Our Ambitions

The more ambitious we are, the more susceptible we are to stress. This is not to say that all ambition is bad. There is merit in striving for excellence, striving to become the best possible person and minister we can be. The good steward found out that "to whom much is given, much also shall be required."

Yet in this culture ambition can so easily go astray. The drive for money, power, and success consumes many of us to a greater or lesser degree. Our efforts to make more money, know the right people, and attend the right social events can complicate our lives to the point where we've lost track of what's really important to us. Coming to terms with ambition can be a deeply spiritual issue, requiring us to deal with the basics of what our lives are all about. Many people are unclear about what they really want for themselves. So, subconsciously they continue to strive for the things that our culture says are so important. Later, when they have attained these things and realize they aren't what they want, it may be too late to try another path.

Clearly, unchecked ambition can be hazardous to your health. That next job or position may be your undoing. In 1980 I wrote an article called "Your Next Job May Kill You."[1] Pope John Paul I had recently died after less than a month in office. Coincidentally, the article was published right after the death of Dr. Paul Carnes, who had served less than two years as president of the Unitarian Universalist Association. Given those two incidents, I did some informal investigation. A top administrative officer of the National Offices of the United Presbyterian Church USA also had died less than one year after assuming office. The Episcopal Church reported that between forty and fifty percent of newly elected Bishops experience a major physical or emotional illness in the first two years of their new role.

I'm not saying unhealthy ambition was the culprit in all of these cases. Obviously, some church executives will thrive under the stress of a new job, while the same job will kill or make others seriously ill. The point is, if we want to be ambitious and strive to take on more responsibility and more complex roles, then we need to know whether our lives are whole and healthy—physically, emotionally, and spiritually. If they are—Godspeed. If they aren't, let's support each other in getting our lives in better shape before we embark on new ventures. Let's also support each other in being happy and content with our current roles and positions. The truly happy person is the one who wants, more than anything else, what he already has.

CHAPTER 23

Routes to Detachment

Stress can lead to burnout when we remain attached to an emotional load for too long. It just wears us down. When we can't get our minds off stressful subjects, our bodies continue to pump adrenaline into our system and the stress can become destructive. All of us need one or two activities that captivate our minds and energies completely, thus allowing us to detach temporarily from the parts of our lives that are destroying us. Some routes to detachment are:

1. **Hobbies**—woodworking, making model airplanes, refinishing furniture, rebuilding cars, collecting stamps, managing an aquarium, birdwatching, knitting, gardening, reading, crossword puzzles, wine-making, baking, sewing, model railroading, etc.

2. **Sports**—tennis, golf, racquetball, squash, handball, swimming, canoeing, white water rafting, mountain climbing, hunting, fishing, bowling, curling, football, softball, volleyball, sailing, surfing, scuba diving, skiing, spelunking, snorkeling, kite flying, square dancing, running, gliding, sky diving, horseback riding, etc.

3. **Arts**—opera, museums, art galleries, plays, musicals, jazz concerts, dance concerts, choirs, concerts, movies, poetry readings, etc.

4. **Reflective/Expressive Work**—journal keeping, poetry writing, singing, dancing, performing, painting, sculpting, macrame, flower arranging, corresponding with family/friends, etc.

All of these have been significant routes of detachment for some, transporting them from misery and pain into joy and self-fulfillment and, in the process, probably adding years and quality to their lives.

Most of the energy we put into fear and worry is wasted. Both emotions have very important functions—to call our attention to something. Like an alarm clock waking us in the morning, fear and worry call our attention to things in our lives that we need to attend to. Once they have done their job, however, we need to shut them off. To continue to worry or be fearful is as stupid as letting an alarm clock ring all day. When we've done all we can or know how to do, then we should put fear and worry aside. To continue only wears us down physically and emotionally.

Stopping the tendency to worry is easier said than done. Often worry continues even when we tell it to stop. Routes to detachment work to absorb us so completely that we cease worrying. When Jesus was crucified and laid in a tomb, the disciples stewed about it all day and night. Finally Peter said, "I'm going fishing." It was as though he had done all the worrying he could do, and it was time to forget for awhile and do something else. Most of us would serve ourselves better if we would knock off the worrying much sooner and "go fishing."

Creative solutions to complex problems often emerge when people let go of them and move on to other things. In detaching and letting go, we somehow allow new perspectives to emerge. Creativity often requires time and space to germinate and grow. People who are doggedly determined to solve a problem often cannot see the creative alternatives before them.

The most popular American escape is television. Given all the alternatives above, it is a poor route to detachment. It may get our minds off certain subjects for a time, but it is rarely either relaxing or satisfying. Instead, there is often something on TV to remind us of our worry. We sit passively and experience a whole range of emotions, yet we never have to commit ourselves. TV drains us emotionally without giving us a sense of self-worth or a capacity to cope with life. Once the off button is pushed, we feel as empty as the screen.

Think about those activities that have completely absorbed you in the past. Can one of those routes to detachment allow you to escape on a regular basis? If it costs some money, it's probably worth it. Because worry and anxiety can shorten your life and destroy your health, it should be worth something to you to have an escape.

Go for it!

PART FIVE

Implications for Ministry

CHAPTER 24

Spreading the Word:
Self-Care Works

If all clergy were to take the challenge of self-care seriously, they would be different people, more content and joyful people, to be sure. But I believe the impact of a commitment to self-care reaches far beyond the lives of individual pastors. I see intentional self-care as a vehicle for change, not only in our hurting congregations, but in a battered world. I would challenge you to put into practice some of the things you have learned about self-care in helping those around you acquire the wholeness that seems to elude them.

I hope you will feel yourself called to a new kind of healing ministry. Of course, any effective ministry will have a healing impact on your congregation and on your community. But I would like you to visualize yourself in an expanded healing role, one that is concerned not only about people's spiritual and emotional well-being, but their physical well-being as well. I want you, as pastor, to reclaim your role as a medical practitioner in today's world. Perhaps you will feel a call to help mend the artificial division that has been created between medicine and spiritu-ality. At one time, the two areas were bound together; today physicians and clergy rarely confer with each other in efforts to restore people to health. Our parishioners and hospital patients suffer from this false division. Having learned something about health and wholeness in your own life, you are in a position to challenge the status quo and push for a more wholistic approach to the healing arts.

I would also like to enlist you as an advocate in the wholistic health movement. Current medical practice is not wholistic, even though many people believe we are moving in that direction. I believe the medical model, where physicians and surgeons respond primarily to pathology, is more entrenched than ever. Clergy who know something about their own health and wholeness have much to offer the wholistic health movement and can be powerful advocates in their own ministries. Wholistic medicine is one of the few viable options available for solving our current health crisis. Yet there's no natural movement away from the medical model. Wholistic health needs strong advocates who are convinced of its value. As clergy, we need to find other professionals who come at healing wholistically and join them in promoting this approach to physical, emotional, and spiritual health.

I believe medical practice in this country is in real trouble and will probably get even worse. If medical costs continue to outstrip inflation, our health system may crumble under the weight of its own excesses. We need to move from dealing with health problems after they've become acute to preventing acute problems in the first place. Much of medical practice today is aimed at delivering people from the excesses of their lives. Two-thirds of our citizens refuse to exercise. Despite the health warnings, a third continue to smoke. Most of us continue to consume unhealthy food. We are bringing disaster upon ourselves and then demanding that our doctors rescue us when we get sick. Preventive medicine is not even in the picture because we have no way of funding it. And doctors continue to feel justified in escalating their fees.

This country needs a national health plan. Doctors and hospitals will have to accept some type of regulation. Because of our intimate connection with people who are recipients of medical care, we are in a key position to be advocates of realistic yet effective health care practices. Do you feel a sense of call to heal medical practice in this country?

Expanding our healing role in our communities, helping to repair the breach between the spiritual and the physical, becoming an advocate of wholistic health care—all of these roles are part of what I think it means to be in the health and wholeness business. We are to be concerned not only about the health and wholeness of individuals in our parishes, but also the parish system in which we work and the society at large. We are to be about healing the environment in which our congregations and parishioners function. It's all part of being an agent of Grace in a wounded world.

In the last two chapters, I'd like to explore with you how we might reclaim our role as healers and how we might become effective advocates for a system that promotes health and wholeness.

CHAPTER 25

Reclaiming the Clergy Role in the Healing Arts

As a parish pastor, whenever a doctor entered a hospital room while I was visiting a parishioner, I immediately excused myself. I over-valued the doctor's role in making my parishioner well and under-valued my role. On the other hand, I certainly did not receive much indication from medical doctors that they considered me a colleague in the healing arts. Many clergy have forgotten, or simply do not acknowledge, that there is a spiritual and emotional component to physical healing. So we basically relegate the healing role exclusively to physicians and surgeons. I get angry when I realize how much we as clergy allow the medical profession to trivialize our role in the healing process. How quickly we have bought into the notion that we have no business playing with the "big boys."

The Artificial Split

In early religious traditions, the resident holy person was the medical specialist as well. In ancient Shamanism and some Native American traditions, religion and medicine were seen to be cut from the same cloth. Faith healers, both today and in the past, have connected Christianity with the physical realm. Unfortunately, faith healing has gotten a bad name because of some who tried to bilk desperate people out of their money. These charlatans have turned off many clergy to the idea of faith healing as a part of their calling.

But we as clergy belong in the business of healing people's bodies as well as their souls. Stated another way, there is a physical component to the healing of people's souls that we need to recognize. All the best medical technology in the world will do little for many people until some healing takes place on the emotional and spiritual level. When people lack the will to live, medical professionals are up against a barrier that all the best scientific insight cannot surmount. Doctors and nurses, whether they realize it or not, desperately need our involvement in the healing of these patients. When we fail to become engaged with parishioners at this point, we abandon them to their fate. By becoming engaged with them, I mean something more than having a pleasant conversation in the hospital and then closing with some Scripture and a prayer. If these patients have lost their will to live, that's our concern. We need to try to get at the roots of that loss. That loss of hope may have to do with their beliefs about themselves, their families, or the world. If that isn't a spiritual issue, I don't know what is. We must not abandon this work to medical professionals because they are not trained for it and do not see it as part of their job. And to turn this work over to psychiatrists is no better; we are still abandoning a key part of our role as religious authorities.

I do not mean to imply that we clergy should go off by ourselves and do our healing thing in opposition to medical practitioners. A faith healer who claims that all a person needs is more faith, not a good doctor, is perpetuating the artificial split between the body and the spirit, too. We always need to work at the healing side of our role within the context of sound medical advice. I am suggesting that we reclaim our role in the healing arts by becoming an integral part of the healing team in medical facilities. With the possible exception of medical missionaries, the role of medical specialist and spiritual director probably will never again be combined in one person. What is needed in our current scene is a greater acknowledgement on the part of both professions that their work constantly overlaps and that we must work as a team.

The Connection Between Inner States and Physical Illness

Dr. Bernie S. Siegel, M.D. in his bes tseller, *Love, Medicine & Miracles*,[1] unabashedly talks about the inter-connection between medicine and faith. He teaches his clients how to listen to their bodies and give their inner selves healing messages through meditation, visualization, and relaxation. Siegel makes no bones about the healing capacity of happiness and peace of mind. He also claims that unconditional love is the most powerful stimulant of the immune system. "The truth is," says Siegel, "that love heals." He is currently president of the American Holistic Medical Association and has started ECaP (Exceptional Cancer Patients), a specialized form of individual and group therapy based on "carefrontation"—a loving, safe, therapeutic confrontation that facilitates personal change and healing.

Does Siegel sound like a medical doctor who has turned into a faith healer? He does to me. In his book, Siegel refers to a research study that documented the connection between prayer and healing. The researchers were surprised to discovered that prayer not only helped those people who knew that others were praying for them while they were in the hospital, but it also helped those who didn't know others were praying for them. (In this double-blind study, the researchers did not know which group was the test group or that the research was testing the power of prayer.) When Siegel posted the study on the bulletin board at the hospital in New Haven where he practices surgery, someone scrawled "bullshit" across it within an hour. Siegel is not popular with some of his fellow physicians and surgeons. Yet I know of clergy who would pass the same judgment on this study. Some of us have become so skeptical about the connection between faith and healing that we have stopped looking for openings to healing in our physically ill parishioners.

Seven years ago, my own mother, Frieda Oswald, was diagnosed as having cancer in her lymph glands (lymphoma) at age seventy-nine. At the time I was reading the Simontons' book and was struck by their research documenting the connection between meditation and visualization and the rise of a person's white blood cell count. My mother began using Simonton's method of visualization: she imaged tiny ants systematically carrying away her cancerous cells. She also was a person of deep faith and continued the prayer life she had practiced all her adult life. That process, plus massive family support and radiation treatment, did the trick. She has had no recurring symptoms. In the summer of 1990 we gathered in Manitoba to celebrate her eighty-sixth birthday.

Becoming a Faith Healer

Lawrence W. Althouse, a United Methodist minister, holds a regular healing service in his church. And for this reason, Larry gets some pretty

shabby treatment from his colleagues in mainline denominations. Larry
is perceived as a regular guy—more intellectual than emotional, more
liberal theologically than fundamentalist, more inclined to approach any
religious matter from a rational perspective—but on the subject of healing, Larry is considered a pariah. One time a close colleague actually
said, "Larry, why's a guy like you doing a thing like this." The "like
this" indicated that, because he thought the two of them shared the same
theological label, he assumed that they would both show disdain for the
practice of spiritual healing.

Larry did not always believe in the legitimacy of a healing ministry.
A careful study of the New Testament convinced him. He discovered
that roughly one fifth of Matthew, Mark, Luke, and John is concerned
with Jesus' healing ministry. Furthermore, he found that the scriptural
basis for the ongoing ministry of healing was very sound. Jesus actually
did send his disciples out to "preach, teach, and heal." And the ministry
of healing continued after Jesus' resurrection and the founding of the
Apostolic Church (see Acts 3-4, 9, 14, 16, 20, 22, 28.) Paul listed healing as one of the specific gifts of the Spirit in 1 Corinthians 12:9, and the
apostle James makes a point to instruct the church:

> Is any among you sick? Let him call for the elders of the church,
> and let them pray over him, anointing him with oil in the name of
> the Lord; and the prayer of faith will save the sick man, and the
> Lord will raise him up...(James 5:14-15)

Larry also discovered that the Greek word *sozo*, which in English
we invariably translate as "to save," may just as rightly be translated "to
heal or make whole," and that the Greek word *soter* means both "savior"
(as we usually translate it in English) and "healer." Thus salvation does
not mean simply the rescue of the spirit but the bringing of wholeness
wherever we are broken. Christ's ministry, therefore—as well as that of
his church—is a healing, saving ministry that seeks to restore wholeness
to mind, body, and spirit.

After much more study, thought, agonizing, and prayer, Larry
finally went to his official board and proposed this new ministry for the
church. To his surprise, the proposal was approved almost without
discussion and with no dissent. On Thursday morning, January 16, 1966,
Larry held his first healing service. Since that time he has had no end of
surprises, most of them positive. A regular group in the parish prays for

healing and receives requests from around the country. Larry has a folder full of letters of gratitude for the healing that has taken place as a result of this ministry.[3]

Larry's story should be an encouragement to the rest of us mainline Protestant clergy that healing ministries belong in our congregations along with the ministries of the Word and sacrament. We need to rid ourselves of the notion that only the "weirdo type" clergy engage in this type of activity. We are missing out on a truly relevant and helpful way to minister to and with our people.

In time of serious medical crisis, parishioners often look to their clergy to be a channel of healing from God. I believe clergy who are willing to receive these projections and respond accordingly can be channels of healing. By this I mean clergy who are willing to learn to become more comfortable in physically laying their hands upon parishioners at the time of their illness or pain and intentionally praying for them. Faith healers quiet their minds and allow themselves to become a channel of Grace for the individual, so there's no room for ego trips. If any healing takes place, it is a gift of God and to be recognized as such. Rather than getting hooked on the process, we need to be open continually to the mysterious connection between faith and physical healing.

In this process, the healer first employs a mental technique to quiet his or her mind. The healer feels a sympathy for the patient and tends to 'blend in' with him or her. Says Lawrence LeShan, M.D., in *The Medium, the Mystic, and the Physicist*,[4] "There is no attempt to 'do anything' to the healee, but simply to meet him, to be one with him, to unite with him." In other words, the prayers and encouraging words as well as a quieting calmness during the healing process may encourage the person's belief system to begin to break the harmful loops of thinking and anxiety cycles that are hindering recovery or causing illness. Whether healings by spiritual healers are a result of the placebo effect or outside forces or energies probably can never be determined. Medical knowledge and technical expertise simply are not sophisticated enough to measure this.

Whatever the causes of healing, I have been positively surprised and pleased with several clergy colleagues from mainline congregations who have quietly begun afternoon or evening healing services in their congregations. The Reverend Carole Crumley, Canon at the Washington Cathedral, began healing services in St. Joseph's Chapel at the Cathedral several years ago. She talks of how exhausting this ministry can be as people really do come to project their illness onto participating clergy, expecting a miracle. Yet she also tells of how rewarding it is and how she has learned volumes about ministry as a result of those healing ministries.

I pray that many more of us will take the plunge and reinvest ourselves in a ministry that is rightfully ours and needs our participation—the healing arts.

CHAPTER 26

Clergy as Advocates of Wholistic Health

Whether or not I have convinced you to engage in the ministry of the laying on of hands, I hope I can encourage you to become an advocate of wholistic medicine. For clergy, this role involves helping parishioners understand that good health is no accident but rather a result of the choices they make about how they will live. You are in the position to help them see that lifestyle has more to do with longevity than magical medications or surgeries. We need to wean people from the notion that they can live a precarious lifestyle, indulging in excesses on a regular basis, all the while expecting medicine to give them the magic bullet—a pill, a by-pass operation, chemotherapy, a facelift, liposuction, a tranquilizer, or ulcer medicine.

In advocating a wholistic view of health we begin with the notion of the individual as an integrated whole, with each dimension—physical, emotional, intellectual, social, spiritual—inextricably bound to each other. We may focus for a short time on a physical manifestation of an illness, but to treat that symptom in isolation from the social, emotional, and spiritual dimensions is to miss an opportunity to effect long-term healing. Wholistic medicine began as a reaction to our classic Western approach to medicine. In this country, we believe that one must know and understand the separate components in order to know the whole. So our medical researchers spend much of their energy dissecting things. They break things down into microbes, viruses, bacteria, molecules, atoms, etc. There is no question that this western approach to medicine has contributed substantially to the health of individuals not only here but around the world. But today I believe the medical model is too narrow for acquiring and maintaining the kind of wholistic and long-term health we all desire.

While we in the Western world devoted ourselves to the medical model, the Chinese proceeded in a totally different direction. Because the Chinese have been isolated from the rest of the world, their approach has had little influence on Western medical research. The Chinese believe that in order to understand how an organism functions you must observe it in its context. People get sick, they say, because they live in unhealthy environments. So they help people create environments that are more conducive to health. From a spiritual point of view, they teach people to be in harmony with themselves, their environment, and the universe. They have developed many social norms that guide people into respecting one another's harmony. For example, it would be quite improper to say something confrontational in someone's home because this would destroy personal and family harmony. So the Chinese focus on studying the inter-connectedness of everything. The concept behind acupuncture, for example, is balancing the various elements in the body so they can work together in greater harmony.

When Chinese and western doctors meet, they must work very hard to understand each other's viewpoint. Each side is working from a different paradigm, and each has a lot to teach the other, but I think the Chinese approach to medicine is much more wholistic than the western style.

Fundamental to wholistic medicine is the recognition that health requires a consideration of all contributing factors: psychological, psychosocial, environmental, and spiritual. For example, research consistently demonstrates that the quality of the environment is a primary determinant of the general health of any population. Prior to the industrial revolution, epidemics and plagues were the major cause of disease and death. At the turn of the century, cholera, tuberculosis, dysentery, and typhoid were beginning to abate but not because of increased medical efficacy. Improvement in agriculture, housing, sanitation, nutrition, water purification, and sociopolitical equality played the decisive role in improving the general health of the population and increasing longevity. The oft-cited exception to this is the development of antibiotics and vaccines between 1935 and 1955, which led to the further control of infectious diseases such as pneumonia and polio.

As the threat of infectious disease receded, a whole new set of disorders, often called the "afflictions of civilization," began to rise rapidly, namely cardiovascular disease, cancer, arthritis, respiratory disorders including emphysema and bronchitis, and depression. These disorders, often related to stress, have shown little decline in incidence since the turn of the century despite the concerted efforts of medical research and treatment. Measurable advances in these areas have been very slow or negligible. Causes of these disorders seem to reside in factors such as stress, genetic predisposition, unhealthy environments, and especially lifestyle. I believe that if the majority of people in our culture changed their lifestyles, we would see a dramatic reversal in these afflictions. But there is much resistance to making such changes.

At present, we have no comprehensive system of preventive care in this country. In an anthology of essays entitled "Doing Better and Feeling Worse," John H. Knowles, the late president of the Rockefeller Foundation, gathered twenty experts to focus on the present crisis in medical care. Overall, the essays acknowledge unequivocally that the effectiveness of medicine is limited, with its greatest efficacy in diagnosis rather than treatment, and that health care is largely a matter of individual initiative. Ultimately, the solution to the present crisis in health care involves individual responsibility. We must curtail our self-destructive behavior—what we often call the "good life." Among the destructive habits in question are overeating, smoking, dependency on medication, reckless driving, lack of exercise, excessive consumption of alcohol, and excessive stress with poor coping strategies. Knowles suggests that the basic assumptions behind this destructive behavior are: 1) a denial of death and disease coupled with the demand for instant gratification and the orientation of most people in most cultures to live day by day, and 2) the feeling that nature, including death and disease, can be conquered through scientific and technologic advance or overcome by personal will.[1]

The Wholistic Difference

Wholistic medicine not only tries to view every individual with a medical problem as a unique individual, but it also tries to relate any disorder to particular psychological and behavioral information. In our current medical system, patients' verbal accounts of their illnesses often are ignored. Physicians rely almost entirely on laboratory assessment. We as patients evaluate our health differently from medical doctors. We may

use "feeling well" as a criterion for health, while medical doctors use an
absence of symptoms as the key criterion. Also, health may be defined
differently by different patients. Factors such as age, education, socioeconomic background, and family of origin need to be taken into account
yet often are not.

Wholistic medicine takes very seriously the relationship between the
patient and the health care specialist. When trust and caring do not flow
both ways there may be serious problems in both diagnosis and treatment. The doctor and patient must spend time getting to know each
other better. Yet in most of our clinics and hospitals, where patients are
viewed as a mosaic of interchangeable parts, anyone competent can treat
that person. The relationship is less important.

Wholistic medicine also recognizes the role of stress in life and its
interaction with a perceived illness. Any diagnosis of a disease that does
not also take into account the individual's stress is incomplete because
people return to the same environment or lifestyle that created the symptoms in the first place.

A wholistic approach to the healing process also views medicine as
only one aspect of health care. Health is not seen merely as a sub-
specialty of medicine. Unfortunately, state licensing laws allocate the
practice of medicine solely and strictly to licensed physicians and surgeons. A variety of other health care professionals may deal with a
patient's particular needs only as defined by a physician's diagnosis.
This makes it very difficult to redefine health care away from the treatment of disease and toward the maintenance of health. It's biomedical
"Catch 22": wholistic practitioners who attempt to broaden the scope of
health care are legally limited to working within the pathology model
that focuses on disease rather than health.

Kenneth R. Pelletier believes a better model would have physicians
as the sole providers of medication and the sole performers of surgery,
but working alongside other health care providers who would help the
patient with prevention, lifestyle modification, psychological counseling,
and general support.[2]

In the next decade this nation will be struggling with how to provide
affordable and quality health care. I believe the current medical model
will begin to crumble under the weight of its own excesses. Many
physicians and surgeons will be loath to give up their time-honored role
as the kingpins of health care and their high salaries. But, nevertheless,

alternative health care models will spring up over time. Local congregations can be part of this grassroots movement.

Two Specific Recommendations

If you are interested in knowing more about this grassroots movement, I encourage you to become more informed about wholistic health and the wholistic movement. Subscribe to at least one magazine that promotes disease prevention and wholistic health. Following are my favorites:

Medical Self-Care, P.O. Box 10572, Des Moines, IA 50347-0572. Six issues for $11.97 as an introductory offer, approximately seventy pages per issue.

Health Confidential, Box 53408, Boulder, CO 80322. Twelve issues for $49.00 per year, approximately eight pages per issue.

Also begin to search out the wholistic health professionals in your community for both personal and professional support. Perhaps you will be able to find more complete health care for yourself—and some people who are willing to view you as a partner in the healing profession. You then may be able to refer parishioners when it seems appropriate.

The Church Moves into Wholistic Medicine

A Lutheran colleague, Granger Westberg, has been pioneering in this field for the last twenty years. He began pressing for a more wholistic approach to medicine while working at Lutheran General Hospital in Park Ridge, Illinois. In a speech at a clergy conference, Granger gently jested with clergy about how important they must feel to have so many people to visit in local hospitals. Granger said he often wanted to ask clergy, "What is not happening in your congregations that results in your having so many who are sick in hospitals." In a sense, he was saying that a healthy congregation assists its members in staying healthy; sick congregations make people sicker.

In one sense this statement may be unfair. There are so many other factors that can contribute to health or illness. But it's certainly something to look at. If many people in a congregation are physically ill, perhaps the chief decision-making body needs to consider if these illnesses might be grounded in negative experiences people are having in the parish or in the community. Passivity in the face of illness is not the best stance for either a congregation or an individual.

When Granger Westberg began his efforts toward a more wholistic health system, he tried to include local clergy as part of healing teams, along with physicians, surgeons, and nurses. But clergy usually felt intimidated and peripheral to the healing process in medical facilities. And the doctors could not or would not grasp the concept of such teamwork, even though they admitted that the majority of patients suffered more from psychological and spiritual afflictions than physicial ones.

Granger then began to experiment with this same kind of teamwork within a parish context. A physician, nurse, pastoral counselor, and receptionist worked together in the church building and gradually they became a close knit team. Through a grant from the Kellogg Foundation, Granger began to set up Wholistic Health Centers around the country.

Though we may not be able to go as far as Granger did, we can take significant steps toward promoting wholistic health in our parishes. First, we need to begin thinking about ministry wholistically. For example, when a parishioner is ill we will automatically know that the illness may be caused by stress from any of the five dimensions—physical, emotional, spiritual, intellectual, social. If the stress is in the spiritual dimension, it may arise from problems of perceiving, valuing, and believing. Each sickness has a particular meaning: this symptom at this time creates this kind of disorder in the total context of life. Getting sick can be an escape or an act of asking for nurturing or an abdication of responsibility. Exploration of the meaning of the illness for a person is crucial to the return to health and prevention of illness in the future. As clergy we can often be helpful to parishioners when we ask such questions as: "Why are you ill?" "Why are you ill now?" "What does this illness symbolize for you?" "What would you have to let go of to relieve this illness?" The search for the meaning of illness often serves as a source in identifying just where in life people are "stuck" and what they need to let go of in order to get moving again—in order to regain health. Within the balance of the whole person, spiritual values are often powerful resources for health. Faith (commitment to something beyond self) acts as an energizer, vitalizer, and mobilizer of personal resources.

Disease can be a warning signal that spurs people to examine habitual patterns of living or personal beliefs and adopt new attitudes and behaviors more conducive to health and wholeness. Wholistic health practice invites individuals to tune in to signals of dis-ease when first experienced, attend to them, and respond with movement toward health, rather than waiting until the dis-ease renders them dysfunctional.

As you can see, the pastoral counselor's role as part of the healing team is central. We as clergy can help people focus on how they feel about themselves and the stress they are experiencing, how they view their faith and the quality of their relationships. We can be especially vital in relating people's stress to their health (or illness) and in assisting them to see the centrality of spiritual issues in coping with stress. Helping people gain clarity about their aim in life, their beliefs and values, and what they choose to spend themselves on can be key in their understanding of health and illness.

The ultimate goal of wholistic health practice is to engage the patient in his or her own care. Patients are asked to choose their own treatment plan and to think about ways they might normally sabotage such a plan. Then the patient works with the team to develop strategies to safeguard against such tendencies. It is the patient, after all, who lives with his/her body; she or he must be encouraged to bring all resources to bear on the healing process.

Redefining Wellness and Sickness

As wholistic health advocates, we clergy are helping to redefine what we mean by wellness and sickness. Health is not the opposite of sickness. Health is the ability to deal creatively with the problems of life—to confront them, withstand them, cope with them, grow from them. We are healthy when we are able to cope with the problems and flux of life in responsible ways. Thus health is a positive force rather than the absence of illness.

Viewed from this perspective, healing is a movement toward wholeness. The goal of healing is not a return to the status quo, but a more complete, higher form of health and wholeness. Physical disease and other apparent calamities of life (pain, suffering, aging, death) can be seen as valuable and meaningful events in life if wholeness can be attained through them. Through the process of healing, people can become healthier, more resourceful, more creative, and better able to manage life, cope with change, and make their own decisions than they were before the "illness."

Thus healing becomes a process of re-creation, bringing new energy, a sense of joy, and the ability to be in process and to change without conflict. The process of healing does not only solve one problem, it is a process of education. It teaches people how to solve present problems and supplies them with the skills for acquiring and maintaining wholeness in the face of future problems.

The process of healing demands attention to the spiritual-depth dimension of life. As a natural course of life people will have gains and losses: the death of a loved one, a job transfer, a new child, a career opportunity. Dealing with these transitions is a major part of the healing process. The return to wellness demands that the old way of life be challenged and new behaviors for expending energy and gaining rewards be adopted. The spiritual process of death and resurrection is always a part of the healing of a person.

The ideal Wholistic Health Center also engages people in an ongoing educational process in which they plan for their future health. It is much less expensive to educate people concerning detection, diagnosis, and management of certain diseases than to care for them when they become disabled and economically unproductive.

The Parish Nurse

Short of sponsoring a wholistic health center in your congregation, a parish nurse may be able to engage you and your congregation in wholistic health.[3] This concept has taken hold firmly in congregations and appears to be growing rapidly. Sixty nurses and clergy participated in a two-day training seminar in 1987; four hundred attended in 1990.

Some parish nurses are employed full- or part-time; others volunteer their services in their own parishes. Generally, these nurses find deep satisfaction working in preventive medicine as their training emphasized this aspect of health care. Granger told me a parish nurse serves five key functions:

1. Health Education

The parish nurse, responding to the needs of church members, schedules speakers and seminars on health issues. Members are invited to learn more about their own health care and how to participate in their own wellness.

2. Personal Health Counselor

Although the parish nurse does little direct medical care, members feel free to talk over their health issues with her or him. The parish nurse may check their vital signs such as pulse, temperature, and blood pressure, but essentially she or he assists the individual in planning next steps in coping with an illness or in maintaining health.

3. Trains Volunteers to Assist in this Ministry

Once the program gets underway, there is more work than can be managed by one person. The parish nurse trains volunteers to help manage the educational events, to visit people convalescing in their homes, to transport people to their health appointments, etc. As more people get involved, the concept of wholistic medicine begins to permeate the whole congregation.

4. Acts as a Liaison with Medical Systems

The parish nurse may brief a physician or surgeon on a church member's symptoms or medical history. When the patient returns from a doctor's visit, the parish nurse may assist him or her in understanding the prognosis. If the visit with the physician was unsatisfactory, the nurse may act as an intermediary to develop deeper understanding on both sides. Generally, the parish nurse is seen as an extention of one of the local hospitals and thus has an inside track in that facility.

5. Integrate Faith and Health

This last function may be the most important. The parish nurse works closely with the pastor to help people understand the body-mind connection and the importance of faith, hope, and love in the healing process. There is a biochemistry to faith. Possibly the parish nurse could participate in periodic health services held in the church.

Of course, before any of this can become a reality in your parish, you need a solid grounding in wholistic medicine. The more knowledge-able we clergy become, the more people in our parish will be drawn into greater wholistic self-care. If we're believable advocates who live out what we preach, others will want to join us in a journey towards wellness.

Living Out the Incarnation

For me, this book has been an exploration, a search for something that can easily elude us. That thing is balance. First, we are seeking a balance between caring for oneself and caring for those people whom God has entrusted to us. Then we are looking for the balance needed to main-tain a modicum of health in four spheres of life: the emotional, physical, intellectual, and spiritual realms. Striking a balance in these areas is the key to effective ministry. Without it, clergy will not be vibrant messengers of Grace. It is as simple, and as important, as that.

In thinking about self-care and balance, the term "incarnation" has taken on new meaning for me. Every human being is a spirit or life force contained or "incarnated" in a body. Each of us must come to terms with how we live within our "soma" or human body. Again, we come up against a paradox, for we must learn to both accept our bodies and con-tend with them. We need to be able to say thank you to the Creator for whatever beauty, grace, and endurance our bodies display. But we also must acknowledge that our bodies have limitations. Because of heredity or environment or our own willfulness, we all have addictions to face and overcome.

The good news is: we can live healthy lives within these human limitations. But it requires dealing with one tough customer—ourselves. Perhaps some of the principalities and powers that the Bible talks about are all those things that tempt us to live in a state of imbalance. It cer-tainly feels that way to me.

So let's continue to support each other in our struggle for balance. Let's do it not only for ourselves but because we love the church. Let's do it because we want to help the church be a more effective agent of healing and Grace to a broken world. After all, this is a kingdom issue. Let's press onward.

NOTES

Introduction

1. These addictions and neuroses include avoidance, denial, projection, alcohol and drug abuse, food addictions, sexual malfeasance, and medication (the three most prescribed drugs in this country are Tagement for upset stomachs, Inderol for high blood pressure, and tranquilizers for relaxation and sleep). See Gerald May's *Addiction and Grace* (New York: Harper & Row, 1988).

2. A small minority of physicians and therapists have caught the vision of a spiritual dimension to personal wellness, e.g. Bernie Siegal, *Love, Medicine and Miracles;* Scott Peck, *The Road Less Traveled;* Norman Cousins, *Getting Well Again;* Richard Moss, *The Black Butterfly;* Brugh Joy, *Joy's Way.* These persons are rapidly filling a void left by church professionals who remain confused and ambiguous about this connection.

Chapter 1

1. Assimilation of New Members study (Washington, DC: The Alban Institute, 1980-81).

Chapter 2

1. March A. Roach, *Competent Ministry* (Nashville: Abingdon Press, 1974).

2. Matthew Fox, *Whee, We, Wee All the Way Home* (Santa Fe: Bear & Co., 1981).

3. Henri J. M. Nouwen, *The Wounded Healer* (Garden City, NY: Doubleday & Co., Inc., 1972).
4. Charles Hollingsworth, *No Foothold in the Swamp* (Grand Rapids: Zondervan Publishing House, 1988).

Chapter 3

1. John D. Adams, *Understanding and Managing Stress* (San Diego: University Associates, Inc., 1980).

Chapter 4

1. T.H. Holmes and R.H. Rahe, "The Social Readjustment Rating Scale," *Journal of Psychosomatic Research* (1967 Vol. 2), 213-218.
2. Alvin Toffler, *Future Shock* (New York: Bantam Books, 1970).
3. C.M. Parkes, *Bereavement: Studies of Grief in Adult Life* (New York: International Universities Press, 1972).
4. C.D. Jenkins, "Social and Epidemiologic Factors in Psychosomatic Disease," *Psychiatric Annals* (1972 vol. 2), 8-21.
5. George Engel, "A Unified Concept of Health and Disease," *Perspectives in Biology and Medicine* (1960 Vol. 3), 459-85

Chapter 5

1. H.I. Russek and L.G. Russek, "Is Emotional Stress an Etiologic Factor in Coronary Heart Disease?," *Psychosomatics*, (1976 17 2), 63.
2. Of the four general areas of pathology that are afffected by stress, the top one, cardiovascular disorders, or the bottom one, imbalances of the immune system resulting in cancer, accounted for 58.3 percent of all the deaths in this country in 1987 (The National Center for Health Statistics).

Chapter 7

1. Introvert and Extravert are references to the Myers-Briggs Type Indicator (MBTI). Some people tend to draw their energy from their inner world and are depleted by too much people contact. These are Introverts. Extraverts tend to be energized by interaction with lots of people. For more on how the MBTI can be used in the church, see Roy

Oswald and Otto Kroeger's *Personality Type and Religious Leadership* (Washington, DC: The Alban Institute, 1988).

2. Herbert Freudenberger, *Burnout: The High Cost of High Achievement* (Garden City, Anchor, 1980).

3. Jerry Edelwich and Archie Brodsky, *Burnout—Stages of Disillusionment in the Helping Professions* (New York: Human Sciences Press, 72 Fifth Ave., 10011, 1980).

4. Christine Maslach, "Burned-Out," *Human Behavior* (Sept. 1978), 17-20.

Chapter 9

1. Marilyn Macholwitz, *Workaholics* (Reading, MA: Addison-Wesley Publishing Co., 1980).

2. "Georgia Halfway House Is Fired Pastors' Haven," *The Washington Post* (July 2, 1990).

3. Robert Sabath, Article on Pastoral Burnout, *Sojourners* (Washington, DC 20017, Box 29272, April 1981).

Chapter 11

1. Barry Johnson, "The Polarity Game: How to Manage Unsolvable Problems," (Washington, DC: Alban Institute Presentation, May 1989).

Chapter 12

1. H. Benson, *Beyond the Relaxation Response* (New York: New York Times Book Co., 1984).

2. Gerald May, *Will and Spirit* (San Francisco: Harper & Row, 1982).

3. Anonymous 19th century Russian peasant, *The Way of a Pilgrim*, translated by Helen Bacovcin (Garden City, NY: Image Books, Doubleday & Co., Inc., 1978).

4. For other good reading material on the discipline of meditation I recommend *The Other Side of Silence* by Morton Kelsey (New York: Paulist Press, 1976), *Living Simply Through the Day* by Tilden Edwards (New York: Paulist Press, 1977), *How to Meditate* by Lawrence LeShan (Boston: Little Bean & Co., 1974).

5. Ira Progoff, *At a Journal Workshop* (New York: Dialogue House Library, 1975).

6. The Shalem Institute for Spiritual Formation, Mount St. Alban, Wash., DC 20016, Tilden Edwards, director.

7. You can contact Roy Fairchild at San Francisco Theological Seminary, San Anselmo, CA. Contact Jack Biersdorf at the Ecumenical Theological Center, 8425 West McNichols Road, Detroit, MI 48221, (313) 342-4600.

8. Tilden Edwards, *Spiritual Friend* (New York: Paulist Press, 1980).

9. You can order "Chants for the Road" by sending $9.95 to Life Structure Resources, Box 212, Boonsboro, MD 21713.

10. For a listing of other chant tapes, write Life Structure Resources, Box 212, Boonsboro, MD 21713 or call (301) 432-6054.

11. To order the Taize tape, send $9.95 to Life Structure Resources, Box 212, Boonsboro, MD 21713 or call (301) 432-6054.

12. J. Goldstein M.D., *Triumph Over Disease by Fasting and Natural Diet* (New York: Arco Publishing); H.M. Shelton, *Fasting Can Save Your Life* (Chicago: Natural Hygiene Press, Inc.); J.F. Wimmer OSA, *Fasting in the New Testament* (New York: Paulist Press, 1982); Dr. Paavo Ariola, *Fasting: How to Stay Slim, Healthy and Young with Juice Fasting* (Health Plus Publications, P.O. Box 1027, Sherwood, OR 97140, 1971); Fr. Thomas Ryan, *Fasting Rediscovered* (Ramsey, NJ: Paulist Press, 1981).

Chapter 13

1. BioDots may be obtained from Life Structure Resources, Box 212, Boonsboro, MD 21713.

2. Johannes H. Schultz, *Autogenic Training: A Psychophysiologic Approach to Psychotherapy* (New York: Grune and Stratton, 1959).

3. Several books, tapes, and videos on hatha yoga are available. If you are new to this discipline, I recommend the book *Yoga 28 Day Exercise Plan* by Richard L. Hittleman (New York: Workman Publishing Co., 1969).

Chapter 14

1. James B. Adams and Celia A. Hahn, *Learning to Share the Ministry* (Washington, DC: The Alban Institute, 1975).
2. A. Richard Bullock, *Sabbatical Planning* (Washington, DC: The Alban Institute, 1987).

Chapter 15

1. Eric Lindemann, "Symptomatology and Management of Acute Grief," *American Journal of Psychiatry*, (1944:101), 141-48.
2. Lisa Berkman, "New Roundup," *Behavior Today*, Dec. 26, 1977).
3. Bruce Reed, The Oscillation Theory from *The Task of the Church and the Role of Its Members* (Washington, DC: The Alban Institute, 1975).

Chapter 16

1. *USA Today*, May 24, 1990.
2. Dr. Larry Gibbons reported these results at a meeting of the American College of Sports Medicine in Salt Lake City.
3. "Health After 50," *The John Hopkins Medical Letter*, (Johns Hopkins, 550 N. Broadway, Suite 1100, Baltimore, MD 21205, October 1990).

Chapter 17

1. We get our bread from Rudolph's Specialty Bakeries in Bristol, Pennsylvania. Call (215) 785-3985.
2. Norman Cousins, *The Healing Heart* (New York: W W Norton & Co, Inc., 1983).
3. For several years I had tried in vain to get my cholesterol level below the 200 level. It was not until I read Robert E. Kowalski's *The 8-week Cholesterol Cure* (New York: Harper & Row, 1987) that I found a way to accomplish that goal. Kowalski recommends the use of niacin, which has the effect of suppressing the liver's output of cholesterol. It's unclear exactly how niacin works to lower cholesterol levels, but it does work for some people. So a regimen that combines niacin, which

controls the liver's output, with a low-fat, high-fiber diet, which controls the intake of cholesterol, is proving to be quite successful.

Chapter 19

1. R. Alex MacKenzie, *MacKenzie on Time* (cassette) "How to Save Two Hours a Day," (Allentown, PA, 18001, Day Timers, 1979).
2. Merrill E. Douglas and Joyce McNally, "How Ministers Use Time," *The Christian Ministry* (January 1980).
3. Speed Leas, *Time Management: A Working Guide for Church Leaders* (Nashville: Abingdon Press, 1978). Other good resources on time management include: *How to Get Control of Your Time and Your Life* by Alan Lakein (New York: Signet, 1973); *Putting It Together in the Parish* by James D. Glasse, (Nashville: Abingdon, 1972); *Confessions of a Workaholic* by Wayne Oates (Nashville: Abingdon, 1971)
4. For more information, contact Ted Engstrom or Ed Dayton at World Vision International, 919 West Huntington Drive, Monrovia, CA 91016, (213) 357-1111.

Chapter 20

1. Rollo May, *Power and Innocence* (New York: W W Norton and Co., Inc., 1972).
2. Robert E. Alberti and Michael Emmons, *Your Perfect Right* (New York: Pocket Books, 1970).
3. Robert E. Alberti and Michael Emmons, *Stand Up, Speak Out, Talk Back* (New York: Pocket Books, 1974). Other recommended books on assertiveness training include: *Don't Say Yes When You Want to Say No* by Herbert Fensterheim and Joan Den Baer (New York: David McKay Co., 1975); *When I Say No I Feel Guilty* by Manuel J. Smith (New York: Bantam Books, 1975); *Assertive Woman* by Nancy Austin and Stan Lee Phelps (San Luis Obispo: Impact, 1970); *Power Analysis of a Congre-gation* by Roy M. Oswald (Washington, DC: The Alban Institute, 1980).

Chapter 21

1. Norman Cousins, *Anatomy of an Illness* (New York: W. W. Norton and Co., 1979).

2. Malcolm L. Kushner, *The Light Touch: How to Use Humor For Business Success* from reading book cassette series, "The Fast Trade," The Best Business Books Summarized on Tape (3000 Cindel Drive, Delrand, NJ 08370, 1989).

Chapter 22

1. Roy Oswald, "Your Next Job May Kill You," *Action Information*, (Washington, DC: The Alban Institute, 1980).

Chapter 25

1. Bernie S. Siegel, M.D., *Love, Medicine & Miracles* (New York: HarperCollins, 1986). Siegel is not the only one who is making the connection between spirituality and physical healing. Dr. Herbert Benson in his two books, *The Relaxation Response* and *Beyond the Relaxation Response* (New York: The New York Times Book Co., Inc., 1975, 1984) cites numerous studies on the body/mind, faith/mind connection. Drs. O. Carl Simonton and Stephanie Matthews-Simonton document the connections between healing visualizations and the cure of cancer in their book *Getting Well Again* (New York: James L. Creighton, Bantam Books, Inc., 1978). Norman Cousins' book *Mind First* (New York: W W Norton & Co., Inc.) speaks directly to this connection as well.

3. For more about Lawrence W. Althouse's ministry, obtain his book, *Rediscovering the Gift of Healing* (Nashville: Abingdon Press, 1977).

4. Lawrence LeShan, M.D., *The Medium, the Mystic, and the Physicist* (New York: Viking, 1974).

Chapter 26

1. J. H. Knowles, *Doing Better and Feeling Worse* (New York: W. W. Norton & Co., Inc., 1977).

2. Kenneth R. Pelletier, *Holistic Medicine* (New York: Delacorte, 1979).

3. Granger Westberg with Jill Westberg McNamara, *The Parish Nurse* (Parish Nurse Resource Center, Parkside Center, 1875 Dempster St., Park Ridge, Illinois, 60068, 1987).

SELECTED BIBLIOGRAPHY

Adams, John D. *Understanding and Managing Stress, A Book of Readings*. San Diego, CA: University Associates, Inc.

___. *Understanding and Managing Stress, A Workbook in Changing Lifestyles*. San Diego, CA: University Associates, Inc., 1980.

Airola, Paavo. *How to Keep Slim, Healthy and Young with Juice Fasting*. Phoenix, AZ: Health Plus Publishers.

Althouse, Lawrence W. *Rediscovering the Gift of Healing*. Nashville, TN: Abingdon Press, 1977.

Benson, Herbert, M.D. *The Relaxation Response*. New York: The New York Times Book Co., Inc., 1975.

___. *Beyond the Relaxation Response*. New York: The New York Times Book Co.,Inc., 1984.

Borysenko, Joan, Ph.D. *Minding the Body, Mending the Mind*. Menlo Park, CA: Addison-Wesley Publishing Co. Inc., 1987.

Carlson, Richard, Ph.D., and Shield, Benjamin, eds. *Healers on Healing*. Los Angeles: Jeremy P. Tarcher, Inc., 1989.

Cousins, Norman. *Mind First*. New York: W. W. Norton & Co., Inc.

___. *The Healing Heart*. New York: W. W. Norton & Co., Inc., 1983.

Dufty, William. *Sugar Blues*. New York: Warner Books, Inc., 1975.

Edwards, Tilden. *Living Simply Through the Day*. New York: Paulist Press, 1977.

___. *Sabbath Time*. Minneapolis, MN: Seabury Press, 1982.

___. *Spiritual Friend*. New York: Paulist Press, 1980.

Ellis, Albert, Ph.D., and Robert A. Harper, Ph.D. *A New Guide to Rational Living*. Hollywood, CA: Wilshire Book Company.

Fox, Matthew. *Whee, We, Wee, All the Way Home*. Santa Fe, NM: Bear & Company, 1981.

Friedman, Meyer, M.D., and Diane Ulmer, R.N., M.S. *Treating Type A Behavior*. New York: Ballantine, a division of Random House, 1984.

___ and Ray Rosenman, M.D. *Type A Behavior and Your Heart*. Greenwich, CT: A Fawcett Crest Book, Fawcett Publications, Inc., 1974.

Glasser, William, M.D. *Positive Addiction*. New York: Harper and Row Publishers, 1976.

Harbaugh, Gary L. *The Faith-Hardy Christian*. Minneapolis, MN: Augsburg Publishing House.

Hay, Louise L. *Heal Your Body*. Santa Monica, CA: Hay House, 1982.

Hittleman, Richard. *YOGA 28-Day Exercise Plan*. New York: Workman Publishing Company, Inc., 1969.

Johnson, Spencer. *One Minute for Myself*. New York: William Morrow and Company, Inc., 1983.

Joy, W. Brugh, M.D. *Joy's Way*. Los Angeles: J.P. Tracher, Inc., 1979.

Kelsey, Morton T. *The Other Side of Silence*. New York: Paulist Press, 1976.

Kowalski, Robert E. *The 8-Week Cholesterol Cure*. New York: Harper and Row Publishers, 1987.

Leas, Speed. *Time Management*. Nashville: Abingdon, 1978.

LeShan, Lawrence. *How to Meditate*. Boston: Little, Brown, and Co., 1974.

Levine, Stephen. *Meeting at the Edge*. New York: Doubleday, Dell Publishing Group, Inc., 1980.

MacNutt, Francis. *Healing*. Notre Dame, Indiana: Ave Maria Press, 1974.

May, Gerald G., M.D. *Will and Spirit*. San Francisco: Harper and Row, 1983.

McLuhan, Marshall. *The Medium Is the Message*. New York: Bantam Books, 1967.

Miller, William A. *The Joy of Feeling Good*. Minneapolis, MN: Augsburg Publishing Co.

Moss, Richard, M.D. *The I That Is We*. Millbrae, CA: Celestial Arts, 1981.

Murphy, Joseph. *The Power of Your Subconscious Mind*. Englewood Cliffs, NJ: Prentice-Hall, Inc., 1963.

Oyle, Irving. *The Healing Mind*. Millbrai, CA: Celestial Arts, 1975.

Peck, M. Scott. *The Road Less Traveled*. New York: Simon and Schuster, 1978.

Pelletier, Kenneth. *Mind as Healer, Mind as Slayer*. New York: Dell Publishing Co., 1974.

Pines, Ayala M. and Aronson, Elliot. *Burnout.* New York: The Free
Press, Macmillan Publishing Co., Inc., 1981.

Pritikin, Nathan with McGrady, Patick M., Jr. *The Pritikin Program for
Diet and Exercise.* New York: Grosset & Dunlap, Inc.

Progoff, Ira. *At a Journal Workshop.* New York: Dialogue House
Library, 1975.

Siegel, Bernie S., M.D. *Love, Medicine and Miracles.* New York:
HarperCollins, 1986.

Simonton, O. Carl, M.D., and Stephanie Matthews-Simonton. *Getting
Well Again.* New York: James L. Creighton, Bantam Books Inc.,
1978.

Toffler, Alvin. *Future Shock.* New York: Random House.

Tubesing, Nancy Loving. *Philosophical Assumptions.* Hinsdale, IL:
Society for Wholistic Medicine, 1977.

Turner, Victor. *The Ritual Process.* Chicago: Aldine Press, 1969.

Westberg, Granger E. and McNamara, Judith Westberg. *The Parish
Nurse.* Park Ridge, IL: Parish Nurse Resource Center.

Williams, Paul. *Das Energi.* Glen Ellen, CA: Entwhistle Books, 1973.

Wimmer, Joseph. *Fasting in the New Testament.* New York: Paulist
Press, 1982.